#UntitledTwo

#UntitledTwo

Neu! Reekie! Publishing #2

Edited by
KEVIN WILLIAMSON and MICHAEL PEDERSEN

Polygon

First published in Great Britain in 2016 by Neu! Reekie! Publishing
and Polygon, an imprint of Birlinn Ltd.

Birlinn Ltd
West Newington House
10 Newington Road
Edinburgh
EH9 1QS

www.polygonbooks.co.uk

ISBN 978 1 84697 353 6

British Library Cataloguing-in-Publication Data
A catalogue record for this book is available
on request from the British Library.

The publishers acknowledge investment from
Creative Scotland towards the publication
of this volume.

Design and typesetting by Gerry Cambridge
www.gerrycambridge.com

Printed and bound by
TJ International, Padstow, Cornwall

Contents

Acknowledgements & Thanks

WE'VE MADE IT TO *#UntitledTwo* which means something has gone right. No two guys are an island and this project underlines what a vast network of talent is around us. We'd like to thank all the writers and artists who've generously contributed to this publication. Salutations! Special thanks once again to Edward Crossan, Alison Rae, Vikki Reilly and everyone at Polygon for their patience and persistence in helping push this publication into the light. To Gerry Cambridge once again, our font of knowledge, for his sterling work and advice on design and typesetting. To Creative Scotland who have supported Neu! Reekie! and helped us make things happen, including this project. To our friends in whisky, Stephen Marshall and Ziggy Campbell, for many things, not least for getting us on the road in the summer of 2015 and maltily slaking the public's drooth. To Summerhall for their continued support. To new recruit Kat Gollock—welcome aboard the N!R! cavalcade, let's get marching. But biggest thanks of all go to everyone who's come along to our events, whether as performers or audience. Your encouragement, feedback and occasional shenanigans are invaluable. Lang may it continue. As we said in *#UntitledOne* print publications are important but when push comes to shove Neu! Reekie! is primarily about the live happenings, where we can engage directly with artists and audiences. Again, thanks to everyone who's helped spread the word, helped out at events—especially Gavin Fraser and Mike Lithgow who've been with us from the start—or helped connect us with so many interesting artists and venues. That was a bit cut-and-paste from *#UntitledOne* but with added zing and kaboom. Some of these poems may have appeared in print previously and credit is acknowledged in the Contributors' Notes. The necessary licences and copyrights for their publication in *#UntitledTwo* have been sought out by the individual authors—please contact us for further details or queries regarding any specific work.

Kevin & Michael
Edinburgh
Spring 2016

Twatter: @neureekie
Faecesbook: www.facebook.com/neureekie
Dumb&Dumblr: www.neureekie.com

#UntitledTwo—Mission Statement

'Auden's great asset is his curiosity. Unlike Eliot, he is not (as a poet) tired…
he reads the newspapers and samples ordnance maps. He has gusto, not
literary gusto like Ezra Pound, but the gusto which comes from an unaffected
(almost ingenuous) interest in people, politics, careers, science, psychology,
landscape and mere sensation.'

LOUIS MᴬCNEICE PAID generous tribute to his friend and fellow poet
W. H. Auden as he highlighted the attributes that helped Auden
establish his mark. The same qualities, it has been said, could also be attrib-
uted to MacNeice himself. Both these men were inspired by everything from
the quotidian to the cosmic, the political and social to affairs of the heart.

With *#UntitledTwo* Michael Pedersen and I have tried to gather together
within these pages a selection of poetry that reflects our own curiosity about
the world and everything in it.

There is no Neu! Reekie! School of Poetry. We try to keep our channels
open, inclusive, provocative, fun, whatever. We're not afraid of veering
towards the experimental or even sailing close to the pretentious. As the
great Howard Devoto once said: 'Pretentiousness is interesting. At least
you're making an effort. Your ambition has to outstrip your ability at
some point.'

There are no rigid boundaries in this book. There is no carving up of poetry
into spoken word versus the page. There is no arbitrary exclusion of those
who primarily put their words to music. The poetry here does not draw from
the life experiences of just one social class. The poetry we've selected, like
all good poetry, is for the ear and for the eye, and for the mysterious layers of
consciousness that draw from poetry what they will.

I'm curious about a lot of things. Especially how and where people read
poetry: alone, together, in small bursts, in long sessions, intensely, on the
toilet, in the bath, on buses, out loud?

Of course there is no best way to read poetry. That would be absurd. Yet
the words of Alice Oswald, in the introduction to her collection, *The Thing in
the Gap-Stone Stile*, have stuck with me ever since I first came across them:

> I hope no one will read these poems who isn't brave enough to
> read aloud and beat the rhythm in the air; because the rhythm
> is the right level—the gauge of feeling—and without it, you

could mistake the book for something polished or earnest or quaint or nature-ish… So please read the poems very slowly, leaving enough time to turn right round between verses and to click the fingers between lines. Language has to balance.

This anthology of poetry has come together through a process similar to its predecessor. With one exception (the late Sandie Craigie), all the contributors have performed or read their work at our Neu! Reekie! salons. They're an eclectic bunch and we've enjoyed working with every last one of them.

Of our guest contributors only Liz Lochhead featured in our previous anthology. There are two solid reasons for that: 1. Liz was oor Makar; 2. Both Michael and I love her dearly. She's been an absolute gem to work with over the years and we hope that will continue in her post-Makar days.

We're fortunate to have Scotland's current Makar, Jackie Kay, included in here too, with four stunning new and unpublished poems. Jackie is another poet we've grown very fond of working with. Whoever picks them Makars knows what they're doing.

If you enjoy all the poetry in this book then fair play to you. Our hope, like that of most anthology editors, is that you'll lovingly discover a poet or two in here you may not have read before. If that happens then we'll have succeeded in whatever it was that we were trying to do.

All we ask is that you spread the word. Catch us at our events. Buy poetry books, as much poetry as you can afford. Buy poetry books that you can't afford. (But hopefully not from Amazon.)

Trying to hype up poetry doesn't work. It resists hype and thrives elsewhere. It thrives between the cracks, on a love of language, a thrill of the unexpected. Poetry will always find an audience if/where/when there is a passion for making it accessible and relevant.

Relevant to what you might ask? This is the six million dollar question. I'm not convinced that poetry should deliver answers to anything. Or maybe the answers lie between the lines. Who knows.

Enjoy.

Kevin Williamson
April 2016

Alan Bissett

We Are the Radicals

We are the radicals. This is radical.

Don't get me wrong it's a *quiet* radicalism, a *civil* radicalism, the sort of radicalism we can all sit round the table and agree upon, yes?

A 'one-nation' radicalism, if you will. One the whole country can rally behind, rich or poor, black or white.

It's sensible radicalism, practical radicalism, one which does not make rash promises, but which recognises reality.

It's a stylish radicalism. This season's radicalism. Radicalism is the new black.

It's radicalism in the way we do business. It's a radicalism which knows how today's busy consumers think, one which understands markets, and which will give us a higher place in the index of globally-recognised radicalisms.

It's radicalism that rewards those who want to work, but has no time for the feckless underclass.

We are the radicals. This is radical.

It's radicalism which does not like soundbites, but which feels the hand of history upon it.

It's the People's Radicalism, the Queen of Radicalisms, a caring radicalism which does so much for deserving charities, highlighting unfashionable causes, such as dolphins ensnared in fishermen's nets.

It's radicalism which is grateful for the loyalty of Our Boys, sacrificing themselves so that we may enjoy our radicalism, a radicalism we should all pause to soberly reflect upon.

(minute's silence)

It's radicalism which is hotly tipped for an Oscar.

It's radicalism which has *so much going for it!*

It's radicalism which satisfies the criteria of the Research Assessment Exercise in Radical Studies.

It's a radicalism in our viewing habits. More of us, for example, are choosing to download long-running series of quality radicalisms, Sky-plussing our favourite radicalisms or watching them at a time more convenient for us on iRadical.

It's a radicalism which, regrettably, has caused civilian casualties.

It's a radicalism which will force us to confront those who seek to destroy our way of life.

It's radicalism which believes in the ability of people to drag themselves up by their boot-straps and simply get on with the job in hand.
No excuses.

It's radicalism which is riveting from start-to-finish, real end-to-end stuff, with bookings, sending-offs, plenty of flashpoints, some fantastic goals, and, above all, top-drawer entertainment for the fans. What do you think, Gary?

It's a radicalism which you control. After you've heard the views of the judges on this week's radicalism, simply phone or text the name of the radicalism which you'd like to win. Ask permission of the bill-payer. Call charges may vary across region and provider.

It's a radicalism the lavish opening ceremony of which will restore our national pride and reflect upon our shared values and traditions.

We are the radicals. This is radical.

Now get out of our fucking way.

Alan Gillis

Gluttony at the Ale House

After Langland

Now bygynneth Glotoun for to go to shryfte
and carries himself kirkward, his sins to lift.
Fasting on a Friday he goes on his way
past Betty's house, the ale-wife, who bids him G'day.
'What way are you for?' she asks.
'To the holy church,' he says, 'for to hear mass,
then to sit and be shriven and sin no more.'
'I have good ale, my Glutton, and plenty in store.'
'Have you,' says he, 'any hot spices?'
'I have garlic, pepper, peony, chilli slices,
fennel-seeds, fenugreek, dried coriander.'
Then Gluttony goes in, and great oaths after.

Matilda from marketing sits at a table,
Vincent from *Virgin*, who works with fibre optic cable,
Beyoncé the barrister, a plumber, a preacher,
Clarissa the accountant, a primary school teacher,
Cameron the toffee-nosed right-wing hardliner,
Bill the butcher, a barista, a website designer
and Belinda the cake-baker all prop up the bar
with Kevin and Michael who deal in second-hand cars
while Daphne, a dentist looking nervous, is
cornered by Davy from information services
and a heap of undertakers, who rise from their seat
to give Glutton with glad cheer good ale as a treat.

So these malingerers drink their Bishop's Finger
and Betty's cherry wine, which tastes of vinegar.
Bill pours Belinda a Bushmills, a Budweiser chaser,
sings Sally MacLennane and tries to embrace her.
The teacher and Vincent are at board playing arrows
when the preacher offers Daphne his prize-winning marrow.
'Feast! Feast!' everyone calls. 'Bring us chicken tikka,

chapattis, roast beef and tatties, spare ribs and paprika.'
'But it is Friday,' gasps Glutton, 'I'm observing my fast.'
'Eat some pies, you whingeing, manky, minging lardass'
cries the barista. And with that Glutton takes Clarissa's
plate and gobbles up her mutton hot-basted with harissa.

The undertakers are at poker, flashing the Joker,
as Glutton chomps on prawn foo yong and a bowl of tapioca.
Sucking his lips that smack of duck, spinach, yoghurt,
the web-designer's fingers waltz up Matilda's skirt.
Michael phones for a mega-meatfeast-multicheese pizza
while Beyoncé, concerned for her five-a-day, picks at a peach, a
passion fruit, pawpaw, pomegranate and papaya.
'Bollocks to that,' cries Glutton, and stuffs his jowls with jambalaya,
a kidney pie, a fat roasted cock, as Agadoo-doo-doo
stomps from the jukebox. He gorges on mud pie, tiramisu
and a well-judged almond cream fudge, slapping the back of Davy,
who thus dips his beard into his chips, peas, onions and gravy.

Warming up, the plumber slips a gin in Daphne's cider,
sings Hit Me Baby, One More Time, then attempts to ride her
while Glutton sings 'I'll drink a river, eat all I can,
forget all my troubles, tomorrow be damned!'
and the crowd cheers him on, chanting 'Arse man!
Arse man! Does all the things that an arse can!'
when he eyes up Matilda, sees she has three heads,
tries for the middle one, tongues the dartboard instead.
Then Cameron enters the body of a pig
and with his y-fronts, his paper money, his ideals of a big
society, he flings off any principle to which we might cling
as he yells out 'I can fuck everything!'

And so there was laughing and louring and 'Let go the cup!'
Bargains were made and beverages bought
until evensong, when the sun melted on the hill
and Glutton had gulped down a gallon and a gill.
His guts began to rumble like a sow in a slather.
He pissed a pot-full faster than you could say Our Father.
He blew the round trumpet of his wide-rimmed arse
and all who heard that horn let out a curse

and held their breath, dreading they might expire,
wishing their noses could be scrubbed with a sprig of briars.
When he tried to walk he swooped sidewards and backwards
as if tracing the flightpath of a flock of looped birds.

And when he drew to the door he dimmed his eyes
then clittered and clattered on the threshold in a pile.
Vincent from *Virgin* tried to help him get up
but Glutton grimly heaved and spewed up
apples, beetroots, carrots, dates, eels, farls,
ginger, hake, ice-cream, jelly, kippers, lard,
mince, neeps, oats, pears, quince, risotto, speck, tahini,
udon noodles, veal, whelks, xacuti, yum yums and zucchinis
into Vincent's lap, his hair, the bowls of his ears.
There was no hound in all of Hertfordshire,
nor rat, nor alleycat, hungry enough to think
of lapping up that leaving, so unholy did it stink.

With all the woe of this world, his wife and daughter
bore him to his bed, mopping his slops and snaughters.
All Saturday and much of Sunday he stayed horizontal.
When he rose again, his first words were 'Who has the bottle?'
But his wife and intestines reproached him of his sin
and he visited Repentance, for to plead 'I'll join the gym!'
He said 'To thee, God, I, Glutton, am guilty.
I have trespassed with my tongue. I have been filthy.
I'll no longer break my fast with so much as a lettuce leaf
until Abstinence, my aunt, has given me leave.
Yet have I hated her, no-one more have I despised.'
Then came Sloth all beslabbered, with two slimed eyes…

Alan Gillis

The Lice Seekers

After Rimbaud

When red Satans torment the child's head
and he craves the balm of milk-white dreams,
two grown-up sisters come to his bed.
On svelte fingers, their silver nails gleam.

They sit him before a large latticed window
where wide blue air bathes a tangle of flowers,
and through his hair, dank with fallen dew,
work their skinny-boned, spellbinding fingers.

He hears the song of their breath's subtle
rise and fall, scented with honeyed tulips,
made sibilant by the hiss of spittle
on their lips, webbed and whetted for a kiss.

He hears their soft eyelashes swish and flick,
and in his half-dreaming mind's eye
their mesmeric, sweet electric
fingers make the small lice crackle as they die.

Now he's drunk on phantasmagoria
as their tidal caresses recede and return,
he feels, like a wheezing harmonica,
an urge to sigh, an urge to gurn.

Bram E. Gieben

Burn

The banks and ATMs are all closed down,
the shops will only barter for gold teeth and family heirlooms.

Except of course the banks are never closed,
they trade in silent algorithms around the clock

faster than human consciousness can calculate.
That's why I'm burning all my money.

I'm taking it out of the bank,
every penny and pound I can beg, borrow or steal,
because otherwise it isn't real.

I want to get the most liberating effect possible
from burning all my money.

I'm burning all my money because
the devaluation of paper currency is inevitable anyway,
and when they call in my debts, they will only send red letters,

more pointless pieces of paper with no value,
or put me in a jail cell for the crime of burning all my money.

Meanwhile...
The foodbank queues are long and full of mothers.
The welfare state has been sold off to pharmaceutical companies
and property developers.

Everything you pay tax on has been
sold off
to corporations
at a loss,

corporations which display the traits of psychopaths
I won't stand for that, I'm burning all my money.

I'm burning all my money rather than see it bail
out another bank that was too big to fail,
or line the pockets of another banker who should
rightfully rot in jail, and it's not like anyone will care about
my lack of wealth, my empty belly or my mental health,
things will remain exactly the same after I burn all my money.

I'm burning my money in stacks and piles,
I don't need an art gallery to film or frame the act,
it is devoid of meaning,
it is a statement about the futility of protest,
it makes about as much sense as burning all your money.

I'm burning all my money as one in the eye
for every two-car family, every celebrity
who ever appeared on television with a white stucco staircase,
a grand piano, two Porsches and a Ferrari in the drive,
shills for a civilisation with no regard for the weak
which champions mediocrity,
I want no part of that, I'm burning all my money.

I'm burning it to staunch my guilt for
every slave who toiled and built
this edifice in which my parents
bore and raised and trapped me,
this hollow church of shopping malls
with blood and hair upon the walls,
with flame enough I'd burn it all
just like I'll burn my money.

I'm burning it as penance for the waste
I've made of all its products, placed,
for all the cancer I've embraced
for every drug shoved up my face,
those sleepless nights and days in haze,
long up in smoke, just like my money.

I'm burning it because without it I will never be free to die
I light the flame and close my eyes
This grey parade of days will cease if you can't afford them

Burn your money

Burn your money because it makes sense

Burn it because it makes no sense

Burn it like a Buddhist monk protesting the Vietnam War

Burn it like a middle-Eastern oil field captured by Allied forces

Burn it like a wicker man, burn it like a blunt

Burn it like a torture victim, face held over hot coals

Burn it because you will only spend it
on things that will destroy you

Burn it because the things you own end up owning you

Burn it because you need more light

Burn it because you don't own it anyway

Burn it because there is enough food
produced globally to feed
every starving mouth.

Because every day you piss away
the compassion that could
make the world a better place on
pointless paraphernalia, and
obsolescent devices.

Burn it because it is an admission
that everything in this system
is corrupt and degraded,
but it can still do one thing for us.
It can burn.
It can burn.

I'm burning all my money and I'm starting today
I already feel much better now the decision is made
I'm tearing up my mortgage and throwing it away,
kissing the wife and kids goodbye and
walking into the sea
naked,
clutching
nothing
but
a lighter
and a fiver.

You won't see me for dust…
I'm burning all my money.

Caroline Bird

The Impact

There are things they didn't tell you

      about levitation: it affects language,

speech becomes frantic, bubbled; eyes

      swim as if independently alive, hours

vanish like downed drinks. Before you

      can slur 'taxi,' you've floated clean off

The Cliff of Everything, and although

      your little legs pedal valiantly like a

cartoon coyote, even *you* know magic—

      unlike gravity—

        eventually

      wears off.

Ciaran Carson

Sans relâche: Without Respite

Shutters flap relentlessly
a starving creature rips out the seams
of ancient garments
covered in mud and pus
yet the water stays pure
in the stoneware jug
on this night clothed in dreams
of order and of peace.
It's been a long time since the painter
seeing
he'd no longer enough paint
to finish his picture
fell asleep
suddenly the same as everyone.

Translated from the French of Jean Follain

Ciaran Carson

Le pacte: The Pact

Lights blown out
pincers left on the workbench
time passes.
Stubble clings to the beaten earth
of the threshing floor.
Written in murky ink
sealed with black wax
the pact concluded between powers
remains loaded with threats.
The poor child plays with mud
the rich one with sand.
A great sadness spreads
through echoless rooms.

Translated from the French of Jean Follain

Colin Will

Joanne

The waitress in the Puglia hotel
reminded me of the nurse
from The Singing Detective.
Dark eyes, dark hair, slim figure,
always on the move, always
doing things.

I couldn't take my eyes off her,
said so, at the table, and the men said
How can you say that? On your anniversary?
But the women approved, nodded,
good to know at seventy plus
desire can still be kindled,
attraction persists, although memory
fails to deliver the actress's name.

Colin Will

Pictish

I'm a Pict who doesn't want to be painted,
who says no thanks to the tattoo man's needles,
who has never sat on a horse in battle, swung a sword
or shot arrows in anger,
who believes the time for raiding cattle
was long ago, and in another country,
who knows none who died at Mons Graupius,
who could not translate Columba's Gaelic,
but who does not speak the old Brythonic tongue either,
who has no Irish ancestry, no Q-Celtic connections,
who did not carve Sueno's Stone, or any other,
who does not have red hair, but is a carrier,
who has never watched Braveheart, nor ever will,
who is not a Mormaer, broch-builder, crannog-dweller,
who likes Pictish art and imagery, has a silver ring,
whose family came from the land of Ce, but
who knows nothing of the land of Ce,
except it is good farming country,
who knows the hills and straths of his forebears,
and loves them, but does not want to live there,
who feels a kinship with those who work the fields
and tend the beasts, but that's as far as it goes,
who knows no standard to which he will rally,
who believes a people is not a country,
who knows a country is an economic and political unit,
subject to change, and it has, and it will,
who will not stand up for a national anthem,
but who gets misty hearing Caledonia,
who knows that the Pict lands are not in the Highlands,
strictly speaking, and that his family
were never in a kilt-wearing clan but wears one anyway,
who thinks Sir Walter Scott has a lot to answer for,
who likes his morning porridge, but puts sugar on it,
who is still coming to terms with being outed as a Pict
by his DNA, a specific marker in all his cells,
who is as confused by this as by everything else.

Dave Hook

A Union Lullaby

Inspired by Matt McGinn's 'A Miner's Lullaby'

Coorie in wee yin
Coorie in wi me
It's cauld oot there
C'mere and get a heat

Ma arms'll gie yi shelter
And I promise I'll haud yi tight
Dinnae you be worried
I'll keep watch until it's light

There's monsters in the shadows
Wi suits and ties and sums
Just coorie in tae me
So you don't have tae deal wi thum

We'll aw coorie in thegither
Tae keep the wolves at bay
I ken yi 'hink yir too grown up
Tae be treated like a wean

But yir better oot ae harms way
I'm working for us baith
Just to keep you safe
So in the mornin' you can play

Don't listen tae the whispers
About moving on fae here
There's trouble in the distance
Good reason to be feart

You wouldnae last the night yirsel
Dark and wet and cold
Just keep cooried in wi yir eyes shut tight
And I'll never let yi go

Dave Hook

Marsh's Mood

Legs slung sideways
over an empty bath
Sucking air through the side of her mouth between drags
She only smokes when she's high
—lost a year to Methedrone
Doesn't mind the Beatles
but prefers the Rolling Stones
She looked at me strangely when I told her
that'll probably all change when she's gets older
Ma fists clenched so tight
wrists twisted
teeth grinding
eyes unfocused on a space in the mid distance

Eccie headrush for a second makes me shiver
I take another pill
watching tracers in the mirror
I wish I was a Mississippi delta blues singer
then maybe I could wash ma sins off in the river
We trade punchlines
in the June sunshine
It's still afternoon
—there's too much time
Can't make ma body clock work
Tick
Tock
Summer got inside
and made the springs unwind

I'm disassembling the mechanism
Wait
I'm misremembering the hedonism
Stomach left behind like an old tyre swing
Playing the blues on a broken violin

Meanwhile
lasts forever in the portal we flew through
battle rapping
and watching adverts on YouTube
Visiting places that few knew
Bomb some Mandy
then pop to the shop for cigarettes and fruit juice

Good balance is true talent
but few have it
Mine's a vod and coke and a fruit salad
The morning arrives with razor tooth talons
Warning—
the highs that we chase are too gallus

Must of drifted off for a wee while
Hello/goodbye
with a bittersweet smile
Faces appear
from the surroundings in mist
And if you think this story is about you then it is

Gerry Cambridge

Requiem

1st anniversary, 17.08.2011

The thin priest maundered on,
mumbling into the microphone,
telling the jaded stories told
a thousand times before, explaining
them to his small and, you would suppose,
ignorant congregation. It seemed no more
than a stagey amateur bit of theatre
with the tinkle of the bells and the white
and purple robes. And suddenly
swallows were going crazy above
the tall blue-lit cupola,
so loud they drowned out the old man's words
with their bright chirrups and riffs
distracting the ears of the listeners. You

took it for a sign from the dead man who,
in his last days on his spotless hospital bed,
had raised his head to the swallows flickering
out over the Ayrshire fields, then let it fall.

I took it for a sign of earth, the unignorable notes
with all the excitement of Africa
in the flexing bloodrust gorgets at their throats.

Gerry Cambridge

The Nature Photographer
1978

> 'The film emulsion for 35mm colour slides,
> *Kodachrome 25*, was renowned among photographers
> for its brightness, vivid colours, and fine grain.'
> —*Dictionary of Film Photography*

The backlit meadow that
October morning early
was millioned with wet crystal
skinkling into rainbow,
and netted webs of garden spiders strung
from twig to blade to leaf.

Obsessional nineteen, I hunkered,
drenched by the tangling stems,
neck-cricked for the perfect angle
with a Micro-Nikkor scrimped
from power-station hours,
to lock light-weighted gems
in the small bright rectangle—briefly
freed from my head's squalors.
Or so I thought them, then.

I pity that young man
uncertain of his home,
nervy to rinse his mind
clean to start again
in fantasies of order
glimpsed through the cramped pane
where the drops winked and flashed
and the spiders hubbed their lairs.
Life was Kodachrome.

Gerry Cambridge

The Tree

18 September, 2014

I returned from the pencilled cross
by the douce streets in my jacket of Maytime green
ceremoniously worn, and scuffling
through chestnut leaves at the kerb, noticed again
and pocketed for the first time since my teens
the green seed capsule spiked
like one of those world war mines
set afloat for the powering hull,
or a grain of pollen magnified
by an electron microscope, armorial and unexpected
for an end of future flowers.

I brought it home: with a fingernail edge
split the sponge-green and opened it
almost as you would the pages
of a book stiff-spined and yet to be read;
and there in its cream pith
perfectly fitted in the plush casket
the big seed with its pale irregular ellipse
that the stem had grown from. The rest
was polished like fine wood
of a steady table where major ends
would be talked out; turned in my common fingers
and catching the light for its hidden tree.

The HaVeN Dundee & Hollie McNish

This poem uses lines produced by the HaVeN Dundee Writers Group and arranged by Hollie McNish.

Kevin McCabe

You have a boxer's nose, like me
a bruiser—bashed many times
a defender of your own
from the unspoken
scarred and broken
you have travelled the world over
on your beautiful boxer's nose.

You have a boxer's nose, like me
and two curves like a crescent moon
that delve into your cheeks
when you smile
over tatties, mince and cabbage
keeps you regular you say
toilet paper whitey, beige

a naughty grin

a neck of texture
tanned skin

kind eyes, strong hood, shielding the inner soul
defending you from negativity and harsh words
dirty looks and vicious thoughts

You have a boxer's nose, like me
and a naughty grin
ears—fizzy edged from restless sleep
strife and testing
from foods still digesting
or maybe nibbles from your lovers touch

a smile that lights up
in the middle lower lip
as it stretches
in laughter
and stories
about your false teeth
and real life
the first poem you would ever write
at school

your favourite word is gochel
you spit truth on paper through false teeth
You have a boxer's nose, like me
and a naughty grin
you have hens' feet like me
I know those lines of smiles and happy times

the worry between your eyes
two frown line train tracks
taking you back and forth through adventures
the worry between your eyes
all breaks away as you recant memories of simple pleasures

Consideration, thoughts along your brow
with a pulsing crinkly vein
pumping blood

You have a face with life pulsing through it

You have a boxer's nose, like me
a naughty grin
and a memory full to the brim
with poetry.

You haven't even been to sleep.

Helen Mort

Advice

You should wear more make up on account of your muscles,
the ones stippling your bare arms, turning your back to shingle.

But not too much kohl. Not too much lipliner
or you'll look like a drag queen.

You should probably avoid heels with those calf muscles.
Heavy jewellery will highlight the sinew of your neck.

You should be photographed, certainly,
in black and white, climbing an overhang in a pale crop top

or square to the camera for charity,
in sports underwear, arms locked across your chest

and everyone will agree that's strong
and beautiful. You can't argue

with beautiful. You can only nod your head, attractively
like this. You're beautiful on edges, in doorways,

on the brink. You can lead beautiful to water
but you can't let it drink.

Helen Mort

Beryl the Peril

In my badly-drawn version,
Beryl is getting shit-faced
with Desperate Dan,

matching him
with every dripping forkful
of cow pie.

Beryl is outsprinting
store detectives, hurdling
the trolleys outside Sainsbury's.

Her plaits are strings
of sausages. Her thought bubbles
are crammed with asterisks.

At night, she crooks the phone
beneath her chin and lies
about her outfit to strange men.

Beryl has an oak-tree waist
and knitted eyebrows,
Beryl has a jaw

like a paperweight.
I watch her turn into her namesake,
my grandmother—

her crumpled spine,
her folded lung
her punctured smile,

my gran, who chased her brother
with a pickaxe handle, watched
her father gas himself,

who'd draw the final frames
if only she could
grip the pen—Beryl

clambering from the page
reaching the greatest height, gobbing
on us all.

Helen Mort

Diet

My diet is one letter short, we can't stand
the pot belly of the d. My diet is Chinese Whispers
and dried leaves. It is surprisingly versatile.
My diet comes with a free fork. You use it
to puncture yourself like a barbecue sausage
so all the wasted breath comes out of you,
like this. Mine is the Shackleton Diet, you eat
your boots. The Everest Diet, where frostbite
lightens your extremities. On my diet, you can eat
but only with your eyes shut. My diet
is like the wheel of a very small bicycle,
rotating fast. It's the colander diet: you pick
out the gaps and eat them. My diet is
the South Yorkshire Coalfields diet.
It includes nothing but a small apology.
On my diet, you can eat your own
past, very carefully, like nibbling the corner
of a photograph. My diet is the Diet of Worms.
You can only eat religious assemblies
from the sixteenth century. My diet is
the diet of a dancer who can't dance.
My diet is bigger than your diet and that's
what scares me. My diet is self-sustaining.
If you like, you may begin
to eat yourself, slowly,
starting from inside.

Iona Lee

Become the Rain

When I'm sad I'm going to die,
or I'm worried about bombs
and things bigger than myself,
when the strobe lights and the late nights
get too loud
and I have lost myself
I get in the shower.

I'm too tall
for every bath I've stretched out in.
Too much made of elbows
and pink, bare skin that I don't like
to look at.
But I can let the steam soak my mind free
from all that grit and glitter,
all the flirting and flittering,
all the fast pace, heavy bass
'I'm so off my face' neon nights,
and all that city smoke.

I can let the sticky whisky kisses
and all those pointless conversations
in kitchens
wash off.

Burn off bad decisions
with the strong-smelling perfumes
and potions.

The best water
can be found in secret pools.
Not like that big, brash ocean
that waltzes with the world,
spitting tantrums
and swallowing sailors.

I'm too small
for every sea I've stretched out in.
Too much made of bones that break
and breathing.

But I can let the tide lead
and carry me, like I'm blossom
on a breeze.

I am lighter
in the rhythm of the waves
and its consoling to know
that my crying, may,
one day,
become the rain
that I use to start again.

No, the best water
can be found in those secret pools
in Scotland.
Framed by untrodden tangle wood,
warm light and witchcraft.
Those pools where insects fly
just above the surface,
carrying the sun on their backs.

Here, the water hurries
over warm stones, or sits
quiet and content.
Its cold when you jump in,
knocks all the train journeys
and television from you.

Here, it is all green and golden
and I am the perfect size.

Jackie Kay

April Sunshine

When the people who have lived all of their lives,
For democracy, for democracy,
Survive to see the spring, April sunshine,
It's a blessing; it's a blessing.

In the hospital this bleak mid winter,
You were just an old woman;
You were just an old man.

Nobody imagined how you marched against Polaris,
How you sat down at Dunoon—stood up for U.C.S.
Nobody pictured you writing to Mandela
And fifty other prisoners of South Africa.

In the hospital this bleak mid winter,
You were just an old woman;
You were just an old man.

Nobody knew you greeted Madame Allende
Or sang the songs of Victor Jara
Or loved Big Arthur's bravura Bandiera Rossa
Or heard Paul Robeson at the *May Day rally*.

You were just an old woman;
You were just an old man.

Nobody knew you saw all of 7:84
The Steamie and *The Beveller*'s opening nights...
How you cried with laughter!
How you stood up for the Arts.

How you stood up for the Arts!

In the hospital, throughout this long winter, you were just an old woman;
You were just an old man.

How you went to concerts every Friday at RSAMD
And how just last Saturday you were mad
You couldn't march against Trident with Nicola Sturgeon.

You say: *One less missile would subsidise the arts for a century!*
You say: *Which politician will stand up for the arts!*

You would have struggled with your new grey stick!
You would have walked with your poppy red zimmer.
To march against Trident once more,
To march against Trident stridently!

What do we want? You say! Peace in society.
Time has not made your politics dimmer.

When the people who lived all of their lives
For democracy, for democracy,
Survive to see the springtime, April sunshine,
It's a blessing; it's a blessing.

Jackie Kay

Extinction

We closed the borders, folks, we nailed it.
No trees, no plants, no immigrants.
No foreign nurses, no Doctors; we smashed it.
We took control of our affairs. No fresh air.
No birds, no bees, no HIV, no Poles, no pollen.
No pandas, no polar bears, no ice, no dice.
No rainforests, no foraging, no France.
No frogs, no golden toads, no Harlequins.
No Greens, no Brussels, no vegetarians, no lesbians.
No carbon curbed emissions, no Co2 questions.
No lions, no tigers, no bears. No BBC picked audience.
No loony lefties, please. No politically correct classes.
No classes. No Guardian readers. No readers.
No emus, no EUs, no Eco warriors, no Euros,
No rhinos, no zebras, no burnt bras, no elephants.
We shut it down! No immigrants, no immigrants.
No sniveling-recycling-global-warming nutters.
Little man, little woman, the world is a dangerous place.
Now, pour me a pint, dear. Get out of my fracking face.

Jackie Kay

Running Lines

You run across two bridges at the same time:
Wherever you are someone's heartbeat is close behind,

You run to find out what endures
And what's lost, what cannot be retrieved

To discover why you felt so aggrieved
To let go of the grudges, groans, grievances

To forget the old broken promises
The ones made to you, the ones you made.

You run to cross the Clyde more than once
And see how it is now, imagine how it was once

The ships that haunt its water, the river's past, but first:
You start at George Square, the city's beating heart—

Where the City Chambers mirror the chambers of your heart
And up the steep hill (the hill start used to be your art)

Past GOMA and you are talking to your Ma in your head
Just as you pass somebody who shouts *Go Ma go!*

And it makes you laugh, but you can't laugh and run
For too long the way comedians do a running gag

If you did you would find yourself lagging behind.
Do a runner, you think, *run-time error*, enough—desist!

Try to think worthwhile thoughts or not think at all!
Think of the running costs of life, what matters in the long run?

The way you are loved, have loved runs at your side
Like the invisible beloved, or the loved dead.

You run to leave behind the things you left unsaid
The tomorrows you never got to have, the lost words in your head.

You run to remember and you run to forget.
You run to be aware and you run to zone out.

You breathe in, out, in, your beating heart.
Your body does it for you, your blood and bone.

You run to be together and you run to be alone
To take things in your stride, tell your body you won't let it down.

And you run to make your lost daughter proud
So that she runs towards you,

Across the Squinty Bridge, her arms open wide.
And you run so that your father will stay alive.

When you enter Bellahouston Park, you remember
The times in The House for an Art Lover with your father

Your head fills with blooms and leaves of trees
And thoughts empty and slide and elide you

As a different music starts to play in your head
So that when you remember your dead, the lead weight lifts

You realize that it is better to grieve running
Than standing still, just as you thought of the words of Dolores

When you ran past her a while back now
Of how it's better to die on your feet than live on your knees

And your head is clearing and the fog now lifting
You can run down the avenue of trees

All of a sudden and without you realizing, one step at a time
You are nearly at The Finishing Line

Passed the Salt Market, the Briggait, the Clutha
Dear green, dear beloved, dear dead.

All the things you've seen on this day swirling in your head.
The autumn leaves lift like clefs,

And all the things that you have seen this autumn day
Make you see your city as if for the first time, anew

In all its glory as if it was your city's wedding day
Bagpipes playing and all the cheering, *wey hey hey*

Till your eyes at the end are running too
And your tears like confetti, floating

And the breeze is welcome on your face at the Green
And you look up at the old carpet Factory, Templeton's

And everything you have ever been
Every single place you've seen

Congregate to meet you here, toddler, teenager
Middle aged you, you as you are now, here, all of you

And your past is a running stitch or a cross stitch in a tapestry.
You return to it so often it comes undone, needs repaired, renewed.

Don't be downcast, depressed, don't despair.
Come on. You're strong as the Finnieston Crane, still in working order

You have filled yourself with music like the Armadillo
Now you bend over, fold over, like a weeping willow

You are laughing and crying in the city where comedy
Meets tragedy meets comedy meets Charles Rennie

You have runners with you and yet run on your own
Together-alone on this Great Scottish Run.

Running is an art and art makes a city.
When you run your body rhymes with itself, a body-poetry.

There is nothing to compare, nothing that beats
This utter exhaustion, this knackered euphoria

You need a stiff drink but you won't go there.
You are your own whisky-chaser. Your mind's an emporium.

You're done in, dead-beat, full of delirium.
You want your bed. You want to sleep. You want your Mum.

That you didn't come first, didn't come last, matters not.
That you did better than the last time is what will last.

You've been through the race in your head and got to the finishing line.
Now's it time to get real, get ready. This is your starting line.

Jackie Kay

Year Slide

I wrote myself a note,
Put it somewhere I forgot.
Full moons came: little moons left.
Stars trailed the skies, bereft.
A moth came for the candle.
I had no wick, no metal. I lost April.
May, June…August as well.
I was fluttering, scooped, dead bust—
Somewhere on the edge
Of something and nothing, I was
Hovering. I was on the ledge.
Gone it was, all knowledge.
I was a snowdrift, ice melting
I was hard rain falling.

James Robertson

A Shortbread History of Scotland

Hail Caledonia
  Whisky galore
Make it in Livingston
  Lochaber no more

Glasgow's miles better
  A Gordon for me
Pure dead brilliant
  You'll have had your tea

Ceud mìle fàilte
  Come awa ben
Will ye no
  Come back again?

Ciamar a tha thu?
  Awfie no weel
Jock Tamson's bairns
  In the land o the leal

Scotland free or a desert
  The stag at bay
Pay no poll tax
  Scots wha hae

Lead on, MacDuff
  It wisnae me
Up wi the bonnets
  O bonnie Dundee

A parcel of rogues
  The thin red line
Grannie's Heilan' Hame
  For auld lang syne

Haste ye back
  Come on get aff
Muckle fat sumph
  Stupit wee nyaff

Here's tae us, wha's like us
  Made from girders
Lovely biscuits
  There's been a murder

The blood is strong
  Dunsyre Blue
Whaur's yer Wullie
  Shakespeare noo?

James Robertson

An Octet of Trollopes*

*The Trollope is a verse form, usually consisting of short lines of an
unspecified number, in which both the title and one complete line is also
the title of a work by the great English novelist Anthony Trollope
(1815–1882). There are no other rules (e.g. of rhyme or metre) and
no limit to the number of Trollopes any one poet may compose.*

The Way We Live Now

The way we live now
is the way we used to live,
only now we have
more ways of knowing it,
and fewer ways of living it.

He Knew He Was Right

Even when he was wrong
he knew he was right.
Worse, even when

he knew he was wrong
he said he was right,
right up to the moment

he resigned, having found himself
in the wrong place
at precisely the right time.

Kept in the Dark

After the shame
and the loss of face,
the naked guilt
and the fall from grace,
are you surprised
that some would hark
back to being kindly
kept in the dark?

An Eye for an Eye

This is how we resolve
the differences between us:
an eye for an eye,
a tusk for a tusk,
until we go down together,
blinded by justice,
united in hunger,
and choking in the dusk.

An Old Man's Love

An old man's love
is steady, prone (say the uncouth)
to fewer ups and downs
than the love of youth.

An old man is a tightrope walker
balancing weights of joy and woe,
seeing both the end in sight
and time's deep drop below.

The Duke's Children

For the first time in generations
the Duke's children
are likely to be poorer
than the Duke himself.

Luckily they still have
the Duke's paintings,
which they can gift to the nation
in lieu of inheritance tax.

The Prime Minister

It is our custom
not to recompense
the Prime Minister
with a salary greater than
one-tenth of his potential
annual earnings from lecturing
after he has left office.
This, we find, breeds
a proportional sense of
public responsibility.

The Fixed Period

On the grounds of good behaviour
his sentence was reduced by half.
The fixed period
became detached.
Outside, he looked for boundaries,
but they too were gone.
He didn't want to start again
with a clean sheet.
He just wanted to, full stop,
complete

Janette Ayachi

Song

After Allen Ginsberg, 1954

We all carry the weight
     of love lugging our emotional baggage
through loopholes of existentialism
twenty-one grams
     of precious carbochon stones
        and a sack of cilento figs.
     Sure I have been
cobwebbed in a party dress
crowned by a laurel of laudanum
     the cistern of the moon
        flushing my cathartic prose
     of relic and punctuation.
I have raced towards a roulette of visions
recklessly hissing uncut hysteria
     spun around under a helicopter
        of eternal howling moons
     oil-slick like a Frisco seal
boutique mascara smudged to sinew
in the dulcimer disco of night.
     A dull simmer rendered in my chest
        as I faced Eurydice and sacrifice
     then staggered to front final stanzas
that stood in as understudies for the ultimate epiphany.
But love has grieved generations
     many prophecies of desire
        have ended with lobotomies
     of nervous butchered hearts.

        In the whore-house of my heart
     a starry lit city and perfumed
snatches of borrowed time
a stoic crusade of begonias line the windows
     every kiss draped in lubricious fairytale.

But love is this, a weight of wings
lace and vapour, the body sung electric
beguiling itself on filigree and flicker
zip locked in to a chiffon oblivion
the weight of love surpasses everything.
So I discarded the angels, seraphim and sirens
their wings of mescaline, tails of benzedrine
and kiosks of church organs
only the devils mariachis
offered me masticated truth
but I never once resisted love.

Jenny Lindsay

Reckless as a Flood

A love-letter from Julia to Winston Smith, after
George Orwell's Nineteen Eighty-Four.

Reckless as a flood
tsunami force
each thrust
a victory
the climax
a history
til the quiet death of the afterwards
the head on chest
the eyes elsewhere

You say: *The more people you've had, the more I love you. Do*
you understand that? That we, depressed, are the best lovers;
we always think that we're doing it for the last time…Do you
understand that?
I do, my love.

Each climax a victory, a political act.
This is not the world they taught us.
This is not what we learned at our surrogate mother's knee.
The screen blared *Efficiency*
Pragmatic partnerships
Betrayal when necessary

Pft!

We'll defy them til our eyes water,
Nod and smile at the Anti-Sex League department
who are actively making this pornography.
They know nothing but thrust with no victory.
I have joined them,
tied my waist sash tighter with the hint of
out-of-reach that will make them reach
—that made you notice me, my love.

Give me your agency, that little spark.
Take wanting to smash my head in with a rock,
wanting to defile me in ways you've been forced to imagine
through the habitual act of spilling seed alone,
angry, consumed by Hate Week, confused by touch
and the utter absence of love.

Say it. Love.
I. Love. You. Winston.
With your silly, sorry inevitabilism.

The trick is to do what you want and stay alive just the same.

You would throw acid in a child's face for a cause you know
nothing about.

I already know you will betray me.

But for now: this is the real stuff.
This is the Golden Country.
My clothes discarded easily,
our uniforms mere cloth.
There are no Victory products named so
with no hint of irony

And you—you didn't know this. You thought I
fell asleep too easily when you were trying to 'educate' me in your
(sorry, love, your *dreary*) revolutionary thought, but

the trick is to do what you want and stay alive just the same.
And I have lived. I lived in your reckless touch.
This flood. It was enough.
You succumbed to sleep and I
watched you each time, our bodies reflected
in a crystal and glass paperweight.
I watched your face as you slept.

The rats were miles away.

Kathleen Jamie

Ben Lomond

Thae laddies in the Celtic shirts,
                                      a baker's dozen
lumbering all the way to the summit cairn
the hot last Saturday of May
                          as larks trilled
and the loch-side braes released their midgies…

Well, up at the raven-haunted trig-point
(as the sun shone bright o'er the whole lower Clyde)
they unfurled a banner,
and triumphant-sombre, ranked themselves behind it
                                   for the photies,
  'R.I.P.' it read, then the name of a wee boy

they'll never meet again. Ach,
would the wean were playing fit-ba
            on some bonny banks somewhere…

There's no accounting for it, is there?
                   I mean the low road, and the high.

Kathleen Jamie

The Shrew

Take me to the river, but not right now,
not in this cauld blast, this easterly
striding up from the sea
                    like a bitter shepherd—

and as for you, you Arctic-hatched, comfy-looking geese
                                        occupying our fields,
you needn't head back north anytime soon—

snow on the mountains, frozen ploughed clods—
weeks of this now, enough's enough

                        —but when my hour comes,
let me go like the shrew
right here on the path: spindrift on her midget fur,
                              caught mid-thought, mid-dash

Kayus Bankole

Man up, boy, stop fucking crying.
They call this shit initiation.
A school on how to be a man with the main subject: having power.
But as soon as you graduate you still remain a boy.
You have been learning the wrong things.
How can you learn how to be a man when your are learning from boys?
Find love, be vulnerable, show compassion, have empathy, care.
Boy, man up. Choose life, cherish life.
Boy, man up. Think like a woman before you become a man.
Boy, man up.
Come let me teach you.
Boy, man up.

Kevin Cadwallender

Baz and the Impersonal Theory

My fist is just a vessel
Through which my anger passes
But is untouched by it.

What like T.S.Eliot?, I ask.

Didn't he write
That musical 'Cats?'
He replies.

Well yes…or at least the words…

So did he not like cats?

Well yes…I guess so

A bit anthropomorphic…Cats…
He raises a quizzical eyebrow
Which indicates he is very proud
That he has used that word.

A bit, I hesitantly reply

Especially Elaine Paige.

Baz pulls up the golden bough
and uses it as a back scratcher.

Kevin Cadwallender

Baz: A Defence of Poesie

At the school reunion
Which was just an excuse
To try and shag someone
You missed at school

Or so Baz says as he
Miserably hangs around
Pining after the beautiful Ellen.

Or to brag about your car
Or your house or your money

The same old redundant
Arguments and status hang ups.

After the seventh person had sneered,
Poetry? You're a poet? You?
And made the lame joke
About poetic licences
Being like driving licences
And asked me to
Do a rhyme for them.

Baz finally intervened
As his theory was severely
Crushed by Ellen's lack of interest
And he needed to assert some
Machismo somewhere.

You work in a bank don't yer?
We don't ask you to come here
And show us how to be a wanker.

He might be a poet but he's our poet
So fuck right off before I show you
What I learned at the knacker's yard.

The defence of poesie
Can't always be left to poets.

Kevin Cadwallender

Cooking with Marie Curie

Even her cookbook is highly radioactive.
They are kept in lead-lined boxes,
and those who wish to consult them must wear protective clothing.

To make a Nobel prize or two
Take one gram of radium
You may have to find
The money for this in America.

Take from your lab coat
A test tube containing
Radioactive isotopes
And stir in gently

You may see a feint light glowing
At this point, but persevere
It will be worth the effort.

Now, the other ingredients;
Lose a husband tragically,
Have a scandalous affair,
Be accused of being Jewish,
Be accused of being a plagiarist,
Remember accusations
Are not facts and dissipate
Totally under the heat of truth.

Add two new elements.
Two shiny medals.
You may like to donate
These to the war effort
But don't bother as they
Will be refused.

Aplastic anaemia
Will become fashionable
In the future.

Kevin Williamson

Anywhere but the Cities—Durness

You are there and I am here
        plotting our co-ordinates
        from Smoo Cave to An Tobar
        the ratio of distance over time
        divided by two

Like summer visitors to Brigadoon
        we seek an improbable escape
        through gneiss mountains
        crags lochans and sea
        on a four-dimensional map

This crime that crime good times
        a fusion of heart and soul
        it all adds up in the end
        to inevitable grand erasure

Smoo Cave by the way
        is in retrospective retreat
        tunnelling through lime
        to god knows where
        yawning but still awake
        to the erosion of memory
        the cold implosion of time

Ullapool next where you shut your eyes
        to a landscape of icy indifference
        where I sleep in a curated bed
        of whisky craic and birdsong

See that last night in Durness
        the harsh radio crackle
        of a solitary corncrake
        I thought she was you

telling another tall tale
of metaphor and myth
and endless longing
to an empty glass
in a cool deserted bar

Kevin Williamson

Anywhere but the Cities—Stromness

The bright orange beacon
> of the Stromness
> lifeboat
> helps no one

The harbour waters
> are flat enough
> to reflect on
> shapeshifting cumulus
> blond wisps of Hoy
> a jellyfish sun

A pair of lovestruck swallows
> in perpetual motion
> map out the contours
> of slippery stone walls
> rusted iron
> and seaweed ropes

No great auks
> nothing more exotic
> than a herring gull
> chest puffed out
> strutting the quay
> like she owns the place
> and maybe she does

The red stain of death
> on her yellow beak
> a reminder to the shell
> of a former crab
> that hunger has a price
> and each soft sound
> has a note to itself

A trawler's carnivore shudder
      death rattle smoke
      inaudible insects
      with peedie wings
      smaller than my most
      careless thought of you

I wonder if these creatures too
      can hear the gentle
      persistent lap of time

Here in Stromness
      on this day
      the 11th of July
      summer adagio in blue

Liz Lochhead

Another, Later, Song for that Same Dirty Diva

A fictional character, the Dirty Diva. I'd made her up a couple of decades back,
for fun, and that year, for a bit of a bawdy laugh I hoped, I'd sent her song to
the friend that had inspired her with a chance remark…
   But three years ago I met her. For real.
   In Edmonton, Alberta. I was there for this brilliant poetry festival with the poet
laureates from every province in Canada. I had a great time. They'd put us all up
in a chi-chi hotel—room only, no extras—but they'd given us nice fat envelopes
with our 'per diems'. However, once I got fed up with steak and Bloody Mary, or
eggs benedict or florentine for brunch, I got into the habit of taking a few dollars
out of my per diem envelope, and wrapping up warm I'd venture out along
the block to have a breakfast that was both low-budget and low-cholesterol,
in a certain 'Sunshine Café' that was run by SAGE.
   That is: The Seniors Association of Greater Edmonton.
   And here, one morning as I was refreshing my lippy in the Ladies' after my
eggs-over-easy, standing right next to me, there she was. It was her, the Dirty
Diva herself, and it wasn't how she was dressed, it wasn't how well-preserved
she was (cos she wasn't, she looked like a cross between an elderly Bette Midler
and George Melly with a bit of Tom Waits at his most ravaged-looking thrown
in) but oh I recognised her right away.
   She gave me a long look. And this is what it said:

'Just visiting, honey? Dream on…
This, ma darlin, is the ladies' john
Of the Seniors Association of Greater Edmonton
And Ah'm here to tell you, girl, one fine day
You're going to find yourself permanently here in the Sunshine Café
Fitting in perfectly among us old-timers
With the arther-itis and the arteriosclerosis and the
Alz-heimers.
—Which is not my problem, baby—
No, cruel thing is I can *remember* way back when still
Ah'd some ooze in ma cooze
And he'd a leettle lead in his pencil.
OK, these days it's not the same
But give it a little elbow grease and I'm still game.
Though when you are more
Than three-score-

And-ten
It's very fucking unlikely to be raining men.
Soon you, too, will be grubbing round for the last of the
Last of the redhot lovers
'Mong the 'lasticated leisure-suits and the
Comb-overs…

Ah, it was a very good year—yeah back in
Nineteen fifty sumthin when ma sex life was jus' begun
And the fact you *shouldn't* was… jus' part of the fun.
(Oh boy, the joy
Of being underage, oversexed and in the back
Of someone's daddy's Cadillac…)
Soon the swinging sixties
And ooh baby I swung,
Got all the action that was going—
And plenty—in ma twenties when I was young…
'The permissive society'? Remember?
A great club. I was happy to be a member.
Fantastic! Fuck-all forbidden
'N everybody perked up at the prospect
Of bein'
Bed-ridden.

Yes, in sixty-nine it was a very good year…damn fine
For moon-landings and…sixty-nine.
And in the seventies did I slow up a tad?
Not a whit, not a bit of it. Are you mad?
For there was *always* sex-and-drugs and having a laugh—
When 'a selfie' was certainly not a
Photograph.

Ah, once there was
Powder in the powder room—
You could get it on, no bother
And every which way,

When two-in-a-cubicle used to mean something other
Than what it means today.
Remember, before?
When two paira shoes, under one locked door
Signalled sex, illicit and acrobatic?
Now it's likely to be 'a carer' and 'client', geriatric.

Once there were
Pills, poppers,
Downers, uppers,
All on offer—and no lack o
More than a whiff of more than a spliff of that wacky tobacco.
Now ma handbag still harbours drugs of every description
But these days, darlin,
They are all prescription.'

And she snapped her lipstick back in her purse,
Gave me a wink that said: 'Could be worse'.
Yes, she said all this with a single look.
It was eloquent (oh, I could read her like a book).
It said,
'Forget the nips and tucks, they are not the answers.'
And off she hobbled to join her team
Of geriatric line-dancers.

Yes, off she went leaving me alone
Before the mirror in the ladies' john.
It felt a little flat without her,
She left a kinda…absence in her wake.
I sighed and looked around me and then, fucksake,
Saw something I'd never seen the like of, never since
They started dishing out the complimentary condoms in the
Eighties, remember? Yes. Like…after dinner mints?
Well, what can I say?
That day
In the female comfort-station of the Sunshine Café,
There, then, in the ladies' john
Of the Seniors Association of Greater Edmonton,
Bold as brass, gratis and for free
Openly out there on the counter between the soap dispenser and the

Potpourri
Right before my very eyes
Lo and behold, very much to my surprise—
Free incontinence supplies!

Luke Wright

Family Funeral

And so, as sure as seasons, they arrive
these men and women with my father's face,
last seen mid-childhood at some lunch that dragged.
Now old and mono, crunching up the drive—
the Marks and Spencer's suits, the widow's lace,
the pinstriped nephew's iPod buds and fag.

A round of grimaced handshakes then we're in
where swollen sons stoop down to shrunken mothers
and awkward siblings sit bunched in a line.
We pass the yellowed hymn sheets, it begins:
the family cynics look for cracks while others
sit waiting for the warm and formal chimes.

Which come as steady as the carriage clock
which later causes rifts, as a weak-jawed
young, celebrant reveals to us a man
we'd known for years. It's not so much a shock,
the things we'd never learned about him, more
a sense that we should talk while we still can.

And though a maiden aunt looks somewhat shaken
outside there's gentle laughter, no one cries,
a cousin gives his dad a friendly shove,
the children sneak-off, and I can't believe
it's taken me so long to realise
it's not the death that makes us sad, it's love.

Luke Wright

The Minimum Security Prison of the Mind

The food's so good you think you're free
the screws call in, swap jokes, drink tea
and you know where they keep the key
yes, you can walk out anytime
from the minimum security prison of the mind.

Your inner eye roams rural streets,
it falls on copses, fields of wheat
you douse your dreams in sweet deceits:
yes, you can walk out anytime
from the minimum security prison of the mind.

Just one more fag/pill/burger/shot
now smash the mirror, gild your lot
hang tinsel in your cell and cough
yes, you can walk out anytime
from the minimum security prison of the mind.

To be confined is much maligned
it's not as if the Guv's unkind
those bars are blinds, those bars are blinds
those bare black bars are bijou blinds
and you can walk out anytime
from the minimum security prison of the mind.

Better the devil that lurks inside
than dead-eyed fortune's black-eyed bride
it's caution more than fear, besides
you can walk out anytime
from the minimum security prison of the mind.

The sterile reek of piss and pine,
you whistle as you stand in line
you love her / love them / this is fine
and you can walk out anytime
from the minimum security prison of the mind.

Take back the years this place has borrowed
step away from torpid sorrow:
I'm going now…I'll go tomorrow
I'll go tomorrow. I'll go tomorrow.
'Cause you can walk out anytime
from the minimum security prison of the mind.

Martin Figura

Life Support Machine

They've called it a coma
though his thousand yard stare
makes it look like a trance

and his eyes are eclipses
a thin fringe of blue
flaring the outer space

dark of his pupils
and his friends can't help
tapping their feet

to the beep beep beep
Balearic Beat
of the life support machine.

Blinds all drawn
the dayglo green
ghosts the hooded dark.

When the drugs kick in
he picks up the groove
at first no more

than a spasm or a twitch
then his hands
chop shapes from the air.

And when they drop
he's a smile on his face
as the line falls flat on the screen.

Martin Figura

Washing Machine

To you whitest of white goods, usurper
of wash-board, dolly peg and mangled
drudgery, autumn sale ring road retail
outlet item, steel drum beating kitchen
dancer, dry-clean only label chancer,
loose change rattling money launderer,
lonely housewife hotpoint pleaser, YES
YES YES you fast-spin Cyclops, bless
you father stain absolver, shocking
pink white shirt disaster, omo
-sapien bobby dazzler, blue pullover
pulveriser, student's stinking hold
-all holding moaning mother
emphathiser, laundrette punter
mesmeriser, sodding suddy slick
floor-flooder, magic trick odd sock
provider, old grey knicker elastic
stretcher, butcher's apron cold-blood
-letter, man-sized tissue snow globe
shaker, filth and dirt disintegrator,
radiator damp wool feeder, Levi Strauss
blue denim fader, duvet cover
and bed sheet wrangler, ambassador
for washing powder, juddering
goggle-eyed basement beast.

Michael Pedersen

Deep, deep down

is a motion and a yolk,
is a gluttony, a sweet
soup, my neck tight
and craned, is your open
thighs' honeyed wetland,
summer rain, puddling
now rivering towards
my begging tongue—(*shhhh*
she's unhooked herself);
so under covers
is a purring, a hushed
zoom, is singing carols,
is blood quickening,
is yelling like riding
rollercoasters, cheeks
full strawberry flush,
is…*shhhhhhhhh*….is
shhhhhhhh; deep,
deep down

Michael Pedersen

Cannae Sleep

If not for that blasted boiler bellowing
as if hawking up soot and phlegm
or a nettling sensation parading
over freckled skin, if not for
your legs jolting like a wind-up
toy gone bananas or the fact I
hear breath, feel and nearly see
breath at the foot of the bed; if not for
roving creatures smearing
handprints over the damp,
rattling window on which
the moon has painted itself,
I'd be sound asleep, blissfully dreaming,
sculpting plots so gratifying
I'd applaud myself on waking,
remarking *well dreamt kid*
in the manner of a baseball coach
praising an underrated player
whose homer just won the game. If not

for shattered bone
tightening in my right index,
triggering a seeping pain
which sluggishly curls
around breaks that never quite
healed; if not for that second
cup of heaped coffee, abundant
sugar in wine; if not for rock
shock wilderness challenging
far-off vastness; if not for
a lack of mental shelf space
or the storm outside shaking the air
like tambourines, rainsticks and maracas,
the wind, full cantata, torpedoing
trees, howling like an orgy

of giddy banshees, terrifying
the neighbour's darling
kids; or the thought of
missing cats drenched 'n' greetin'
sheltering in doorways,
the meat on them attracting
Thought Foxes; the cinematic
plop of weighty drips plus the clock,
that fucking clock, tick-tocking
though the hands fell off
years ago; if not for unlit
candles wobbling on china
saucers keen to burn
implying they could be
as smoking stars, illuminating
the scuffed boots and cracked pots below; if not
for shapes and figures
swirling around in darkness
like paint splat on water for marbling
paper; if not for my scant body hair
making itself known, gloating
and breeding; if not
for aw that, I'd be sound, sound
asleep; all of that and today's late
rise and the poker-faced
clerk in Tesco that got me
thinking: I've lost many more
morals than I'd care to admit. Yes, all, all
all of that and one last
secret (or two) I daren't even utter
or you'd wake up, sit
bolt upright and that'd be
the end of that.

Patience Agbabi

Unfinished Business

'Conveniently, cowardice and forgiveness look identical at a certain distance.
Time steals your nerve.' —Jonathan Nolan, *Memento Mori*

That night, it rained so hard
it was biblical. The Thames sunk the promenade,
spewing up so much low life.
It's a week since they beat up my wife,
put five holes in my daughter. I know who they are.
I know why. I'm three shots away from the parked car
in a blacked-out car park. My wife cries,
Revenge too sweet attracts flies.
Even blushed with bruises she looks good. She's lying
on the bed, next to me. *Honey, I'm fine.*
Tonight I caught her, hands clasped, kneeling,
still from a crime scene.
I didn't bring my wife to Gravesend for this.
What stops me, cowardice?
None of them, even Joe, has the right to live.
How can I forgive?

How can I forgive
none of them? Even Joe has the right to live.
What stops me? Cowardice.
I didn't bring my wife to Gravesend for this
still from a crime scene.
Tonight I caught her, hands clasped, kneeling
on the bed next to me. *Honey, I'm fine.*
Even blushed with bruises she looks good. She's lying.
Revenge too sweet attracts flies
in a blacked-out car park. My wife cries.
I know why. I'm three shots away from the parked car
put five holes in my daughter. I know who they are.
It's a week since they beat up my wife,
spewing up so much low life
it was biblical. The Thames sunk the promenade
that night, it rained so hard.

Paul Hullah

Yukimarimo (Jerusalem to Jericho)

The Good Samaritan came by, and he reversed the question:
'If I do not stop to help this man, what will happen to him?'
                                             —*Martin Luther King*

Lamed over lowlands my limbs sink like stones.
Stranger, Levantine, support me.
Dark are my Bible dreams, bruised my black bones,
Resting where questing has brought me.

Lonely are we who love leaving too much,
Trapped in departure, past frozen:
Colder than cobalt, blue flowers we clutch,
Old in our colours ill chosen.

High on her hill sleeps my silent princess,
Mute for the prince made to miss her;
Waken her soft, melt her hoarfrosted lips.
Carry me up there to kiss her.

Polly Clark

Elvis the Performing Octopus

hangs in the tank like a ruined balloon,
an eight-armed suit sucked empty,

ushering the briefest whisper
across the surface, keeping

his slurred drift steady with an effort
massive as the ocean resisting the moon.

When the last technician,
whistling his own colourless tune,

splashes through the disinfectant tray,
one might see, had anyone been left to look,

Elvis changing from spilt milk to tumbling blue,
pulsing with colour like a forest in sunlight.

Elvis does the full range, even the spinning top
that never quite worked out, as the striplight fizzes

and the flylamp cracks like a firework.
Elvis has the water applauding,

and the brooms, the draped cloths, the dripping tap,
might say that a story that ends in the wrong place

always ends like this—
fabulous in an empty room,

unravelled by the tender men in white,
laid out softly in the morning.

Polly Clark

Hedgehog

Its leg was not broken. It was not homeless.
It clenched in my hands, a living flinch.
You cannot love so much and live,
it whispered, its spines clicking like teeth.
I hid it from itself in a cardboard box.

Overnight, it nibbled a hole and slipped away.
I cried so much my mother thought I'd never stop.
She said, *you cannot love so*—and yet
I grew to average size and amused a lot of people
with my prickliness and brilliant escapes.

Rachel McCrum

We Brought It to the Sea to Air

We brought it to the sea to air,
to take the salt cure.

We propped it up to peer
through the smeared crust
of the perspex ferry windows.

We laid it out on harbour walls
and in questionable
guesthouse bedrooms.

We sauntered it along promenades,
held it up to watch gulls shoal
above the drag of waves.
We wound it up to Grieveship Brae
and looked down upon the island.

We tried to stroke it smooth
unrise hackles
unruffle worried feathers
pat down raised scales
till all was silver and rainbows
and still it lay there gasping.

On the beach
we performed mouth to mouth
until we could no longer tell
if those were salt crystals
or sand grains
crunching at the corners of our lips.

We fed it ham sandwiches and chips.
We fed it stamina capsules made from
medically dried dead babies.

Though we couldn't say it,
we'd taken it on a guilt trip.

Better slipped into the water between the pier
and the side of a fishing boat.
Better pecked out by gulls.
Better gutted with the mackerel catch,
hosed into a tank of crabs.
Better smothered by kelp,
lacerated by barnacles.
Better sucked under quicksand.
Better the roof finally falls to crush its skull,
better smashed by a falling stone.
Better rampaged by a heaviness of bullocks.
Better the ribs picked clean by bone beetles
than to lie there gasping.

Finally
we let it go to sea.
Watched it nudge away a crisp packet
beneath the sign for
the Eventide Club.

Silently we prayed
that it was buoyed
by something we could not measure.

Ryan Van Winkle

'It was a dark and stormy night'
　　　　　　—Snoopy

It was a dark and stormy night.
The cage was covered
so the bird went to sleep. I switched
the light on, wandered
through the flat house covered
in the dust of a day. Piles
of books lay uncounted and closed
on the carpet among the veins
of maps, the hills I could have climbed
while the sun was open. I counted letters
I should have written on the hill,
the butterfly I might have chased,
locked in a jar, carried home.
For, when the night turned stormy,
I could have said, 'I have done
something. I have run
for beauty. I have begun.'

　　　　*

I could not sleep.
The bird could not sleep.

It was that kind of dark
like a black sheet

drawn over my house.
This is what it feels like

to get older, to lose the veil
of yourself. They say not to look

in a mirror at midnight. You might
you find a ghost there,

a future spouse, your killer
looking over your own shoulder. I look

at my own eyes. Grey as flags
left on a pole too long. I am sure

I graduated from university. I am sure
I had a favorite cartoon and I know

I watched that video till it bled. I know
I would go home after school. I know

there was Mother's ritual folding
of bread. I know I left home,

drank wine without permission, drank wine
with permission and dropped the glass.

I have dropped more
than I'll ever remember.

I cannot make a list
of the things I've dropped.

I know it would remind me
to hold. I know I dropped a light bulb

and I know I was happy
when a silver of glass sneaked

so deep into my foot
I could not squeeze it out,

could do nothing
but accept it as mine.

*

I had to meet someone, a shadow
with my face I had to confront.
There was a storm of broken light bulbs, a storm
of lightning bugs in a jar. There were a million storms
I meant to say to myself while the sun was up,
while the mirror was clear. There was a pile of books
to read or burn or bury and a sliver of night in my foot
I needed to remove.

*

I am more water
than I am light.

I feel more for water,
think more about it.

Delicate water.
Hard water.

A tea cup
of water.

A train
of water.

Some say water
has been frozen

and is at rest
in state-sized lakes

on the dark, quiet side
of the moon.

*

It was dark and stormy and I
was as visible as anyone, maybe
revealed a little by the rain. But she
began to call me Moon as if
I was far away. *Hey Moon, are you*
hungry? C'mere Moon, give us a kiss.

Later, I became Mr. Moon. *Mr. Moon,*
this is serious. We must call a meeting.

*

This was a dark.
This was a good dark.
This was a dark dark.
This was end-of-the-reel dark.

This was a varnished dark, a dark hull
on Death's *Ship of Dark* steering north
into a storm grey as old boot lace,
the color of wolf fur and no red
riding anywhere near so his claws
rapped on my window like rain
and begged, so I wrapped
a blanket round my treasures,
tied them to a stick and went
to where I knew a boat was waiting,
its dark sails beating
a hoary breath in the night.

*

I dreamt I was walking with strangers—candles
in jars. When Lennon bit the sky someone said
there are many ways a star can fall. I saw
a woman pushing her eyes into her skull
and did nothing. I saw flies in a mason jar,
languid and plump as raisins stuck in sugar

and I did nothing. I saw light bulbs explode
and stars giving up to gravity and even when
I saw my mother's hand thunder
a jar of peanut butter to the floor
I did not fetch a cloth, sweep up the storm.
I did not dry her palm of blood or hide
the chipped tile from father. I did not look up
long enough to make a wish. I made no wishes.

I saw a boy send his finger into the sky
on the back of a Roman candle.
I walked right up to Mr. Death and asked 'How
do you like your lazy boy now?'

      *

It was a dark and stormy night. The wine was black.
From the porch I could see waves sharp
as shark fins and everybody was there.
We were always saying goodbye to someone
already gone. And I dropped the bottle
causing a shattered lake on the floor. Much later,
the phone was ringing. They said
it was 1913 calling.

      *

It was dark. It was stormy.
It was the beginning.
It was also the middle
and the end. It was four
panels and eight hundred
pages. It was black
and white and full color
on Sunday. It was copied
with Silly Putty, it was burned
for warmth or lined the bird cage.
It softened the package, smelled

like sparklers on the fourth of July—
our names singed into sky, our fingertips blooming
stars till our names were eaten, our sticks sulking
to ash in our hands. Our time of sparks would hasten
would fucking fly
so shake another from the blue box
until the box is empty, until
the storm emerges, until
we we are old enough to write
our names with more permanent fires, burned
onto skin, onto tongue, onto letters on paper
and all, we imagine, longer than sky.

*

It was a dark and stormy night and I listened for a change
in the weather and counted all the pills that have piled up
in jars and plastic bottles – each one a colored star I find myself
wishing upon as I never wished before. Zinc for libido,
cod liver oil, one-a-day, Vitamin B for the morning after, Vitamin E
for scars and burns, and so many others I collected
without counting.
          Forgotten children, they sit in the back
of the chest. It was a dark and stormy night and I was counting
all the things that could fall, all the things I could pour,
all the things I could leave behind.

*

Stormy night, she says

and dark, I says

and dark, the parrot says

and dark, she says

and we cover ourselves, make a cage

of blankets. *I like to think*, she says,

that this will be

the end of the world.

Tonight the storm

will rise and swallow

everything which can not

or will not float. This futon

will be our raft, the place

we'd swim to in summer

where parents could only see shapes

and not the point pricking

white skin, hid, water slapping

like tennis balls against the side.

She says she is sad

that this will never be the end of the world

that there will be a tomorrow and the day after tomorrow

until the dark and stormy night when the power went out—

when the light bulb exploded in its socket,

when the parrot learned to say dark,

when we built a cage we understood and understood us—

will be yesterday and then the day before yesterday and the decade

before this decade when the sheets were smooth, unwrinkled,

light and white as popcorn and the world was ours and ours

alone. She says she can think of ghosts while holding me close,

she says it does not matter that the world is ending, that shadows

become monsters, that her thoughts are often haunted

by the man I am not. *The man I am*

enjoys being alone at the end of the world with you, I says

The only thing at the end of the world is the end of the world, she says

And shards, I says

Put your slippers on when you get up, she says,

careful what you step on in the dark.

Dark, the parrot says.

Ross Sutherland

Brian Cox Once Blew Up a Prison in Rio in Order to Explain Star Death and the Creation of the Elements (True)

Next season: Brian Cox goes back to Sao Paulo
to smash up a nice family-owned restaurant.

Everything attacked is a metaphor for the universe,
the air shimmering with broken glass.

Brian shatters the owner's hand against the bar,
HEAT DEATH PARADOX written on his bat.

Brian walks backwards, talking to the camera
explaining the time asymmetry of entropy

stuffing his pockets with notes from the till.
'Physics,' he shouts, launching a chair at a waiter.

In the back room, eating beef and onions,
a police officer. Well respected in his community,

he represents the second law of thermodynamics.
Brian kills him. Camera cuts to a CGI rendition

of the big bang, returns to find Brian, four years later,
living in a cramped police safe-house in Luz.

The end of his index finger is missing.
It appears Brian Cox has betrayed many people.

His tongue swollen, Brian talks to camera about 'irreversible
transformations'. Outside, a car-bomb detonates.

Whatever the explosion was supposed to represent,
Brian has long forgotten: a quote from Einstein,

the galactic redshift, a gluon, the Copernican principle,
the negative heat capacity of a black hole.

Zoom in on Brian's terrified face
as he tries to remember the formation of the universe.

A man enters the safe-house and shoots him.
'I thought I understood but I don't!' shouts Brian, dies.

Cut to his funeral. His family, embarrassed,
talking to camera: where did things go wrong?

Perhaps something right at the start. Some deleted scene;
an unlit, corrupted file. Various BBC execs

approach the molecules once known as Brian Cox,
leave gifts of rock and ice, walk home to wonder

if the metaphor has ended, the rain on their hats
like the sound of a Wikipedia page in flux.

Ross Sutherland

Here

The poem begins: *I loved a man in Liverpool*
but he is gone now, and now I am here.

And this 'here' is understood as the man-sized space
occupied by the poet at the time of the poem,

not the 'here' experienced when I read the words
some fifty years later on a flight to Copenhagen.

The poet is not 'here', cramped into standard,
a screaming newborn in the seat one-over.

This Easyjet Airbus inspired no laments
from an ageing poet to his dead gay lover,

even if he observed a likeness to his friend
in the emergency landing procedure cartoon.

'...*but he is gone now, and now I am here*...
watching an Eddie Murphy film in the sky...'

Funny how a word like 'here' persists,
making poems seem closer than they actually are.

Think of all the places these lines have been read:
a classroom, a prison, a toilet, a park,

all of them equal distance from the dead.
Even in a cylinder, high above Denmark,

en route to a festival to watch Patti Smith,
(who is a bit like a dead gay lover of my own)

Kalundborg beneath me, glittering with sadness,
a map of another man's pain.

I can feel the cabin pressure dropping. Thank God
I can never come back here again.

Ross Sutherland

Writing Drunk About Buzz Aldrin

Thinking about
those orange cabins on Herne Hill
and the strange posture of Buzz Aldrin
always one elbow on the table
leaning forward like
he's sharing a secret.
It was both raining and sunny today.
There was a pinkish fiery sky like
gay hell
sorry
and I felt an incredible weight
as I excited the tube station.
It felt as if there was no more
'free time'—
as if the entire concept
had passed into history,
like non-smoking areas.
I think about sex
and when I'm going to die.
I'd like to track down Chris Jolin
who used to threaten me in school
with a hypodermic needle
and hurt him somehow. Even though
he's probably a normal guy now
with a family and all his instruction manuals
in a box-file. I'd still like to come out of nowhere
and head-butt him
maybe in a shopping centre.
I'd grab him by the collar
and pull him into me
the same way Buzz Aldrin
always seems to be falling towards the camera
on documentaries about the moon.
His massive brown anvil face.
I bet sex on top of a hill is good

because you can slightly see the curvature of the earth.
Sex is best when you're thinking,
'haha life is pointless'.
You don't learn something when you get higher up
You forget something
There are no secrets on the moon.
Buzz just never readjusted to our gravity.

Roy Møller

Nina Simone

Young fan Warren McIntyre was plucked from the crowd to dance with the American
singer at her Mayfest show in Glasgow Green on 3 May, 1994.
—Evening Times, *Glasgow, 7 March, 2015.*

You are here now, Nina, so welcome to the party.
When I hear of you I always think of parties.
At a high-ceilinged mess of tongues in 1983
in the shape of My Baby Just Cares for Me
I first heard your affable piano introduction
via pale students under delicate cornice.

You've blown in here from North Carolina,
and your double-whistling daddy is in attendance,
blown in with your perfect pitch, imperfect equilibrium,
your name that changed the day you perfected
your educated take on the devil's music.
For all the blue languor you can drape on a room,

it's not just the wind that's wild, Nina—there's your
churning, cantankerous reputation. But you occupied
the moment, handclaps behind you, the room syncopated
to sublime punctuations—yes I know, yes I know—
murmuring, a pliant congregation. Then a bunch
of flowers, meet and greet and back to crazy.

If you'd had your way you'd have fired more guns
at those whose chattering
cracked your concentration. You would have fired,
exacting retribution for lynched bodies
and hoods and crosses,
the spectral danse macabre. Goddam.

And maybe that's why you were mad, Nina,
mixing brown make-up into your Natural,
hallucinating laser beams, mixing up your relatives.

But I have seen your ivory sparkle
in the cufflinks of the goateed barista
skooshing cappuccino for a blithe generation.

You're as strict and sensual as a scented hairdresser
cleansing my scalp with practised hands,
yanking my neck back to breast and bone china
and burning my head with uncalibrated water.
You'd pull out a cut-throat razor
if I dare to utter that damn word Jazz.

Baby, that's the white man's limiting label.
Don't you know you're hearing black
classical music? It's not just the wind
that's wild, Eunice Waymon. And nearby now
in time and motion, in a big top, in a lost snapshot,
you're dancing with a dazzled young man.

Salena Godden

My Tits Are More Feminist Than Your Tits

My tits are more feminist than your tits
My tits are more feminist than your tits
No. My tits are more feminist than your tits
No. My tits. My tits. No my tits. No my tits actually
My tits are the feminist tits
No. My tits are the feminist tits

Well, my tits are gay tits. My tits are lesbian tits
My tits are minority tits. My tits are black tits
My tits are more black than your black tits
And my tits are more feminist than your tits

My tits are trans tits. My tits identify as being women's tits
My tits have no say. My tits have no voice
My tits have no vote. My tits have no choice
My tits have got no fucking space to be tits

My tits are more feminist than your tits
My tits are more feminist than your tits
No, my tits are more feminist than your tits
The tits are fighting the tits. The tits are fighting the tits

Look at her tits. Look at those tits
Her tits are good tits
Those are some good tits
Her tits are productive tits
Her tits breast fed her babies
Her tits breast feed in public
Look at those tits
Her tits are leaking milk
Those are disgusting tits
Look at those tits

Look at those tits
Her tits are childless

Those tits are just for titillation
Her tits are fake plastic boob job tits
Page three, shame on her tits
Shame on those tits
Look at her tits

Look at those tits
Her tits are ageing badly
Her tits were legends
Yeah, but her tits are scientology tits now
Her tits were seen drunk in public
One tit popped out
I could see some side boob. Side boob
Did you see the side boob? Side boob?
What the fuck is side boob? Side boob?

Look at her tits
Look at those tits
Those are not real women's tits
Those tits don't do the school run
Those tits don't juggle both motherhood tits and career tits
Those are not the tits of a working mum

Look at her tits
Look at those tits
Those tits are active tits
Positive and sporty tits
Those tits are doing a marathon for cancer and tits
For cancer and tits. Let's support the tits
Support your tits

My tits drank gin all night and cried
My tits have been very naughty
Don't judge my tits
Walk a mile in my bra
See how you like them tits

Look at her tits
Look at those tits
Her tits were asking for it
Her tits were begging for it
Those are the tits of a whore!
Slut shame those tits!
Stop. Tits. No
Sign this petition
Sign my Pet. Tit. Tion.
Sign my tits

Because my tits are more feminist than your tits
My tits are more feminist than your tits
No. My tits are more feminist than your tits
No. My tits are more feminist than yours
Bitchy tits. Bitter tits. Cunty tits
Sub tweet tits. Anti tits. Resting bitch face tits
Tits! Tits! Say it out loud: TITS

Those are my sisters tits
We are all sisters and we all have tits
Would you talk to your mothers tits like that?
Think about it. Think about tits. Think about it. Think about tits

Stop abusing the tits
Raped tits. Hurt tits
Benefit cut tits. Vulnerable tits
Her tits have no love
Her tits have no home
Her tits are refugee tits
Her tits are at war
Her tits sit in a prison camp
Her tits are immigrant tits
Drowning in the ocean tits
Tits on opposite sides of the barbed wire fence tits
Murdered tits. Every fucking day. Murdered tits

All tits are equal
But some tits are more equal than others
I think all women should do what the fuck they like with their own tits

To bra and not to bra is not a question
You don't have to be such a dick about tits
I wish everyone would stop being such a dick about tits

Because all we are saying is
Give tits a chance
All we are saying is
Give tits some peace
All we are saying is
Give tits a chance
All we are saying is give tits some
Peace.

Sandie Craigie

Bi-lingual

I speak in Scots, write in English
I speak in Scots, write in English
I speak in Scots, write in English
I speak in slang, write in English
I ought not to write with a Scottish accent
I write in English, write in English
Think in Scots, translate…translate…
How does NOT mean why
How does NOT mean why
Pronounce OU not OO
House, mouse, now, tousey—WRONG
Ja-louse—WRONG
Jalouse—Wrong
Think 'jalouse'—say 'guess'
Think in Scots with an English accent
Resist…resist…
I fight in Scots, I must NOT fight
discuss in English
I must pass in the English language
Pass—fai—resist
Think—don't think—think
I scream in Scots
I am Scots—with an English accent
I am English—with a Scots accent
Must not be proud
must not be loud
bite this tongue
and it hurts
and sometimes

I bleed in Scots
Dream in colour
Write in black and white
…weep in Scots

Sandie Craigie

Coogit Bairns

Hidden still ir the bairns ae the bairns
ae the stoory glen, hidden
like the bastard sons ae the royal mile
neglected in the towse ae yer art galleries
yer style, wir clingin oan by the fingernails

Or a scattered derry fae the square-like schemes
where never a place tae wet yer mooth
we're oot there; in Pilton, Niddrie an the rest
the bairns ae the bairns

Caw us clart or commoner
aye, caw us what ye like
we still belong an ken it
tae this, the city ae wa's
an you there—wae yer face like a palace
yer soul canny match
an you—wide enough, wae yer wallet an language
an you—standin howkin yer bare erse in yer fur coat
ye ken nowt about nowt, but ken this

Wir clingin oan by the fingernails still
fae the ragged nail tae the clart ahind
the desperate, ey wae the luck ae the deil
fae the bridges stane tae the city wa's
fae the womb in the slit ae the Coogit
whether bield or tenement
oor faithers' faithers built it
an wir clinging oan by the fingernails

An a knife-switch in a night's heat
mair desperate than the tears it brings
an the fuckt-up an the hameles
huv history ower you
in the craws-fits ae her eyes

we huv history
in the lines ae the mooth ae the smirk
in the tongue an the fist

An you wae yer words
an you wae yer money
canny fight a power ye ken nowt ae
history
a constant pagger ae
stane an rubble
built oan treachery
spult wae blood
an the sweat an the bones
ae the murdered

At night by the mirk
an the lampposts blinkin
troglodyte, an landlowper
wae ghost in their blood
come oot bi their dozens

Stey in
Stey in an loak yer doors
fir the night is radge
an the gadgies ravin
cowpin an poppin
an the Coogit reelin

Stey in
Stey in fir the night is owers
in the mind ae oor history
radge as it might be
in the city ae wa's
fir the night is owers
fir the night is owers

Sandie Craigie

Terrorism

It's hard ti get roond the place, keep ooty danger
Keep well oot the wye ae things
Ghosts an broken furniture
Constantly crashin
Bruised thighs fae tables, died airms fae door handles,
A coarner slashes mi
Then it goes an hides the waterproof plasters
An the Germaline
Four tubes a've boat in three months an they wir never
            seen again
How dae ye explain that, eh?
Domestic terrorism
That's aw it is like
Christ, it's even hud a go at aes when am sleepin
Wake up wi that freshly paggered look
'A'll get ye noo, ya fuckin antichrist'
An when a git up in the moarnin,
Or when a cum in late efter bevvyin
A ken ma hoose'll be waitin like a fuckin casual
Ambushed bi irons
An the tie press that prick firgote when he left
An aw the fuckin shite ae the day
A look like a battered wummin
Ma neighbour giez mi a pityin look
A walked inty the door, a say
Bastardin hoose, a say
But she's heard it aw before
'get riddy him' she sez
A widny mind, but a stye oan ma ain

Look up at ma windae, through the clart an stoor
Ye kin jist see the cunts mumblin an mutterin
Square goes noo!
Waitin fir mi
Fuck thum!

Am no gien them the light ae day
If they git their ain wye, a'll huv ti move again, am tellin
        ye though
This time it's war
Men an cleanin!
This time am styin single
An that hoose is gittin its fuckin cunt kicked in

Sophie Cooke

Hermony: The Seein Distance

The distance atween
twa frequencies o soond
is whit perfects thaim,
heard thegither.

Yer stanes cam awa
fae thair cauf-grund tae shape
an airt whance ye micht
leuk back on it.

Nae city's sic a city as it thinks,
no sae faur fae the laund lain aneath it.
Glesgae lilts, at shairp twaloors, tae its redd—
stanes tae their rocks, glass tae its sandy bed—
I cam miles awa fae ye, juist tae fare
the seein distance whilk isnae thare.

Harmony: The Seeing Distance

The distance between
two frequencies of sound
is what perfects them,
heard together.

Your stones came away
from their birth-ground to make
a place where you might
look back on it.

No city's such a city as it thinks,
not so far from the land lying beneath it.
Glasgow lilts, at open noon, to its spawning-bank—
stones to their rocks, glass to its sandy bed—
I came miles away from you, just to travel
the seeing distance which isn't there.

Sophie Cooke

The Cleidin is a Civilisin Mission

Dossed for some place ense—yon Grecian chiffon
can no gainstaund oor snell an blashie wather—
thae hie fowk on oor biggins aye war quarrelled oot'n Scotland:

it wis a faur ben ploy, tae stell expansion
wi bairns, lang-heidit men an dochtie caryatids:
bowsome bodies help tae humanise an Empire's architecture.

Sicna slicht: no tae feel the wecht we cairy,
an that we're stickit; no tae leuk at whit's aneath or
leuk wi unseein eyes, douce white, wyteless plunkers;

receive the peyment—grapes, corn, televisions—
like it war a seilie accident o Naitur.
We aye uphaud hame's structure, a cause o it's a shelter,

but scug an airn will that it wadna mak a god oot o a greedy principle,
an feel wir herts like ammonites beat in the stane whaur builders
            pressed thaim.

The Clothing is a Civilising Mission

Dressed for somewhere else—that Grecian chiffon
can not withstand our sharp and rainy weather—
those high folk on our buildings were, all the same, quarried out
            of Scotland:

it was a popular trick, to prop expansion
with children, shrewd men and saucy caryatids:
obedient bodies help to humanise an Empire's architecture.

The art's like this: not to feel the weight we carry,
and that we're stuck here; not to look at what's beneath or
look with unseeing eyes, sweet innocent white marbles;

receive the payment—grapes, corn, televisions—
as if it were a happy accident of Nature.
We still hold up home's structure, because it is a shelter,

but hide an iron wish that it wouldn't make a god out of a greedy principle,
and feel our hearts like ammonites beat in the stone where builders
        pressed them.

Wayne Price

The Lovers

Late afternoon; the light in weak solution
washes up against the windowpane.
It has travelled a long way from the sun.

Outside, across the promenade, three floors down,
you can hear the chained Atlantic Ocean
raking the shingle and rattling back again.

The lovers are sleeping. You can almost
see them—bodies and minds like clothes undone—
as passengers here, carried by dream.

How they resemble us, or anyone, those faces
blank with exhaustion. Hard to tell them apart:
they have been two, and one, like a mind

that can't be made up. And now everything
is still. No sound. The clock's black arms,
that have no strength of their own,

are not waving them back, or waving them on.
None of it seems to happen in time.
And beyond the window where the sun falls in

the whole weight of the sea flips a shell as thin
as a fingernail, or the lovers' breathing skins.
Late afternoon. Almost evening.

The nuclear boiling of storms on the sun
candles the bedroom's dust in suspension.
The lovers are sleeping. Never wake them.

Wayne Price

The Moustache

The crabs in the bucket
were always exhausted by noon,
had given up the frantic
scraping toward the rim.

It is late afternoon. My brother
carries the catch, winkled out
of the Porthcawl rock-pools
with a flake of tinned salmon.

I see us walking between
the twin rows of caravans,
a family, at least in name,
trailing one behind the other.

My parents are not speaking,
have not spoken since morning;
something about the new moustache
my father—a handsome man—is growing.

Soon we will reach the door of our own
long tin can of fears and spites.
It waits for us, baking
in the last of the heat. Silence for now,

like the crabs' exhaustion.
We'll leave them on the step when we go in.
We don't mean them harm
but they'll be dead by morning.

Notes on Contributors

ALAN BISSETT is a novelist, playwright and performer from Falkirk. He now lives in Renfrewshire. His novels include *Boyracers* (Polygon, 2001) and *Death of a Ladies' Man* (Hachette, 2009) and his theatre work is gathered in the anthology *Collected Plays* (Freight, 2014). Alan will be performing his 'one-woman show' *The Moira Monologues* at the Storytelling Centre during the Edinburgh Fringe, 2016.

'We Are the Radicals' is previously unpublished.

ALAN GILLIS is from Belfast, and teaches English Literature at the University of Edinburgh. His poetry collection *Scapegoat* (2014) followed *Here Comes the Night* (2010), *Hawks and Doves* (2007) and *Somebody, Somewhere* (2004), all published by The Gallery Press. He was chosen by the Poetry Book Society as a 'Next Generation Poet' in 2014.

'Gluttony at the Ale House' and 'The Lice Seekers' are previously unpublished.

BRAM E. GIEBEN has performed poetry across Scotland as a solo performer and as part of Chemical Poets since 2005. In 2015 he won the Scottish Slam Championship and brought his debut solo show #EXNIHILO to the Edinburgh Fringe.

'Burn' was previously published in the collection *ExNihilo* (Weaponizer Press, 2015), and is available on YouTube as a short film at www.youtube.com/texturemusick. A musical version can be streamed at: texture.bandcamp.com.

CAROLINE BIRD is an award-winning poet with four collections published by Carcanet Press: *Looking Through Letterboxes* (2002), *Trouble Came to the Turnip* (2006), *Watering Can* (2009), and most recently, *The Hat-Stand Union* (2013). She was awarded an Eric Gregory Award in 2002, and has been shortlisted twice for the Dylan Thomas Prize. She is also a playwright, currently writing *Dennis the Menace: the Musical* for the Old Vic.

Her poem included here is previously unpublished.

CIARAN CARSON has published some two dozen books of poetry, prose and translation, most recently *From Elsewhere*, translations from the work of the French poet Jean Follain, paired with poems inspired by the translations (Gallery Press, 2014). He is a member of Aosdána, the affiliation of Irish artists, and is a Fellow of the Royal Society of Literature.

Both his poems included here are previously unpublished.

COLIN WILL was born in Edinburgh and lives in Dunbar. One of the 1960s Edinburgh Beats, he later became a scientific librarian. He chairs the Board of StAnza, and has had eight poetry collections published. He's a former Makar to the Federation of Writers (Scotland).

'Pictish' was previously published in *Northwords Now*, and is reprinted with permission.

DAVE HOOK writes rhymes. Sometimes Dave Hook calls himself Solareye. Sometimes he raps with Stanley Odd. Mostly he makes stuff rhyme.

Both his poems included here are previously unpublished.

GERRY CAMBRIDGE is a poet, critic, editor and print designer with a background in natural history photography. His five books include *Notes for Lighting a Fire* (HappenStance Press, 2012), and *Aves* (Essence Press, 2007): prose poems about wild birds. For twenty years he has edited *The Dark Horse* poetry journal. He specialised in British nature as one of the youngest ever regular freelancers (between 1983 and 1988) for the magazine *Reader's Digest*, which then sold in the UK 1.5 million copies a month.

'Requiem', 'The Nature Photographer' and 'The Tree' are published here for the first time.

HELEN MORT lives in Sheffield. Her first collection, *Division Street,* was published by Chatto & Windus in 2013 and won the Fenton Aldeburgh Prize for best first collection. Helen's work has also been shortlisted for the Costa Prize and the T. S. Eliot Prize.

'Advice' was first published in *Alpinist* magazine. 'Beryl the Peril' and 'Diet' are both in Helen's next collection, *No Map Could Show Them*, published in June 2016.

THE HaVeN WRITERS GROUP is a collection of writers who attend sessions at The HaVen Centre in Dundee. They attended a workshop with Hollie McNish as part of a Neu! Reekie! and Edinburgh International Book Festival-run programme in 2015. They were fantastic.

HOLLIE MᶜNISH is a UK poet who straddles the boundaries between the literary, poetic and pop scenes. Hollie has won the Arts Foundation Award (2015), was the first poet to record an album at Abbey Road Studios, amasses millions of YouTube hits and wows audiences all over the world, online and off. Her most recent work *Nobody Told Me* (Blackfriars Books, 2016), a poetic memoir of parenthood, has swiftly became a sensation—'The world needs this book' (*Scotsman*).

IONA LEE is a writer, performer and artist, or at least she hopes to be all of these things soon but she is still in her infancy. Iona began performing spoken word at seventeen; now a student at the Glasgow School of Art, she often illustrates her work. She won the title of Scottish Slam Champion in 2016.

Her poem 'Become the Rain' is previously unpublished.

JACKIE KAY was born and brought up in Scotland. *The Adoption Papers* (Bloodaxe, 1998) won the Forward Prize, a Saltire prize and a Scottish Arts Council Prize. *Fiere* (Picador, 2011), her most recent collection of poems was shortlisted for the Costa award. Her novel *Trumpet* (Picador, 1998) won the Guardian Fiction Award and was shortlisted for the IMPAC award. *Red Dust Road* (Picador, 2011) won the Scottish Book of the Year Award, and the London Book Award. She was appointed the Scottish Makar in March 2016.

'Extinction' and 'April Sunshine' have been published in *The Empathetic Store* (Mariscat, 2015). 'Extinction' was also published in the *Guardian*. 'Running Lines' is published here for the first time.

JAMES ROBERTSON is a writer of fiction, poet, editor and essayist. His novels include *Joseph Knight* (Fourth Estate, 2004), *The Testament of Gideon Mack* (Penguin, 2007) and *And the Land Lay Still* (Penguin, 2011), and his short stories appear in *Republics of the Mind* (Black and White, 2012) and *365: Stories* (Penguin, 2014). His new novel, *To Be Continued*, will be published by Hamish Hamilton in August 2016. He stays in Angus.

'A Shortbread History of Scotland' was first published in the pamphlet *When the Ile Rins Oot* (Kettillonia, 2014).

JANETTE AYACHI is a Scottish-Algerian poet who has been published in over sixty literary journals and anthologies, including *New Writing Scotland, Gutter, The Istanbul Review, Magma, Oxford Poetry, Be the First to Like This: New Scottish Poetry, Out There: Anthology of LGBT Writers* and *The Best British Poetry 2015*. Her pamphlets are *Pauses at Zebra Crossings* and *A Choir of Ghosts*. Janette also edits the online arts journal *The Undertow Review* and performs her poetry across the U.K.

Her poem 'Song', included here, is previously unpublished.

JENNY LINDSAY is a writer and performer of spoken word, based in Edinburgh. She is one half of literary cabaret duo Rally & Broad and has published two pamphlets and one full collection of poetry. Her debut solo show *Ire & Salt* (2015) received four stars from the *Scotsman*, which called it 'Defiant, eloquent, inspiring…full of hope, humanity and humour.'

Jenny's 'Reckless as a Flood' was first published in *Ire & Salt* (Stewed Rhubarb Press, 2015) and also appeared in *The Orwell Society Journal* (December, 2015).

KATHLEEN JAMIE's poetry collections to date include *The Overhaul* (Picador, 2012), which won the 2012 Costa Poetry Prize, and *The Tree House* (Picador, 2004), which won both the Forward prize and the Scottish Book of the Year Award. Kathleen also writes non-fiction including the highly regarded *Findings* (Sort of Books, 2005) and *Sightlines* (Sort of Books, 2012). Her most recent collection, *The Bonniest Companie,* appeared in 2015. Kathleen is Chair of Poetry at Stirling University (part-time). She lives in Fife.

The two poems included here are in *The Bonniest Companie* (Picador, 2015).

KAYUS BANKOLE is a founding member and guiding light of the internationally acclaimed band Young Fathers.

'Untitled' is published here for the first time.

KEVIN CADWALLENDER lives in Edinburgh. His nine collections include *Baz Uber Alles* (Dogeater, 2004), *Colouring in Guernica* (Red Squirrel Press, 2007), *Dances with Vowels: Selected Poems* (Smokestack, 2009) and about thirty pamphlets including *Baz Poems* (Rebel Inc., 1993), *Dog Latin* (Calderwood, 2009). He runs the 10RED poetry event in Leith and is a former Scottish Slam Champion.

His poems included here are previously unpublished.

KEVIN WILLIAMSON is the author of one book of poetry, *In a Room Darkened* (Two Ravens Press, 2007). His babies include Rebel Inc., Bella Caledonia and Neu! Reekie!

Both his poems included here are previously unpublished.

LIZ LOCHHEAD studied at the Glasgow School of Art. *Memo for Spring* (Reprographia, 1972), her first book, brought Lochhead to wider notice at a time when the Scottish poetry scene was largely male-dominated. Her collections of poetry include *Dreaming Frankenstein* (Polygon, 1984), *True Confessions and New Clichés* (Polygon, 1985) and *Bagpipe Muzak* (Penguin, 1991). Lochhead is also a successful playwright, her productions including *Mary Queen of Scots Got her Head Chopped Off* (Nick Hern, 1987) and a Scots-language adaptation of Molière's *Tartuffe* (Nick Hern, 1985). Liz was Scotland's Makar from 2011–2016; she was awarded the Queen's Gold Medal for Poetry in 2016.

'Another, Later, Song for that Same Dirty Diva' is from her new collection, *Fugitive Colours* (Polygon, 2016).

LUKE WRIGHT is the author of eight solo poetry shows. His epic poem/ play *What I Learned from Johnny Bevan* won a Fringe First at the Edinburgh Fringe 2015 and completed a sold-out West End run in 2016. His debut collection is *Mondeo Man* (Penned in the Margins, 2013).
  'Family Funeral' and 'The Minimum Security Prison of the Mind' are from his forthcoming second collection *The Toll* (Penned in the Margins, 2017).

MARTIN FIGURA's new collection *Dr Zeeman's Catastrophe Machine* is out with Cinnamon Press; a show of the same name begins touring in May 2016. The pamphlet *Shed* (Gatehouse Press) is out shortly. His previous collection and show *Whistle* (Arrowhead Press, 2010) were shortlisted for the Ted Hughes Award and won the Saboteur Award for Best Spoken Word Show.
  'The Life Support Machine' was first published in *The Interpreter's House*.

MICHAEL PEDERSEN is Neu! Reekie!'s co-chief/co-founder; he has published two chapbooks and a full collection, *Play with Me* (Polygon, 2013); he's a Canongate Future 40 and a Robert Louis Stevenson Fellowship Award winner. Pedersen has read all over the globe from New York to Tokyo; collaborating with bands, filmmakers and beyond.
  Both poems included here are previously unpublished.

PATIENCE AGBABI is a sought-after poet who celebrates the spoken and written word. Her fourth poetry collection, *Telling Tales* (Canongate, 2014), a contemporary *Canterbury Tales*, was shortlisted for the 2014 Ted Hughes Award for New Work in Poetry and Wales Book of the Year 2015.
www.patienceagbabi.wordpress.com
  'Unfinished Business' originally appeared in *Telling Tales* (Canongate, 2014).

PAUL HULLAH—'silver-tongued devil…journalist, academic, and all-round lush' (*Sounds*)—lived in Edinburgh from 1981–1992, where he was notoriously active in underground arts and music scenes. Relocating thereafter to Japan, he is currently Professor of British Poetry at Meijigakuin University, Tokyo. He has published six poetry collections including *Scenes* (2014), a book/album of paintings, words, and music with Martin Metcalfe and The Filthy Tongues.
  Previously unpublished, 'Yukimarimo' is taken from Hullah's forthcoming volume, *Climbable*.

POLLY CLARK has published three collections of poetry with Bloodaxe Books with a fourth, *Afterlife*, due in 2017. Her novel *Larchfield*, inspired by W. H. Auden's little known but formative years in the Scottish west coast town of Helensburgh, will be published by Quercus in March 2017. Her work has been shortlisted for the T. S. Eliot Prize, won an Eric Gregory Award and twice been selected as one of the Poetry Book Society's books of the year. *Larchfield* won the 2015 Mslexia novel prize. Polly lives in Helensburgh and is Literature Programme Producer for Cove Park, Scotland's International Artist Residency Centre.

Polly's poems are published here courtesy of Bloodaxe Books.

RACHEL MᶜCRUM is a poet, performer and producer of all things poetry. She's lived in Scotland since 2010, coming via Manchester, New Zealand, Oxford and a small seaside town in Northern Ireland. She was the inaugural BBC Scotland Poet in Residence in 2015, and has performed her work in Greece, South Africa, Haiti, Montreal and Belfast. She likes red wine, roll-ups and used to go sailing.

'We Brought It to the Sea to Air' was previously published in *Do Not Alight Here Again* (Stewed Rhubarb Press, 2015).

ROSS SUTHERLAND was born in Edinburgh in 1979. He's the author of four poetry collections: *Things To Do Before You Leave Town* (2010), *Twelve Nudes* (2010), *Hyakuretsu Kyaku* (2011), and *Emergency Window* (2012), all published by Penned in the Margins. He is also the host of the Imaginary Advice podcast. www.rosssutherland.co.uk.

'Here' was previously published in *Sequences and Pathogens* (Litmus Press).

ROY MØLLER, Edinburgh-born, is a poet and late-bloomer living in Dunbar where he helps run the CoastWord festival. His musical entangle-ments include membership of Neu! Reekie! supergroup Jesus, Baby! and he is currently a Broughton Street Sailor. His first poetry collection, *Imports*, was published by Appletree Writers in 2014 and his second, *Carol*, is in preparation.

His poem included here is previously unpublished.

RYAN VAN WINKLE is a poet, live artist, podcaster and critic living in Edinburgh. His second collection, *The Good Dark* (Penned in the Margins, 2015), won the Saltire Society's 2015 Poetry Book of the Year award. His poems have appeared in *New Writing Scotland, The Prairie Schooner* and *The American Poetry Review*. He was awarded a Robert Louis Stevenson fellowship in 2012 and a residency at the Studios of Key West in 2016.

His poem here is from *The Good Dark* (Penned in the Margins, 2015).

SALENA GODDEN writes and performs poetry, fiction, memoirs, radio drama and lyrics. With regular TV and radio appearances Godden has been described as 'the doyenne of the spoken word scene' (BBC, *The Verb*); 'The Mae West madam of the salon' (*The Sunday Times*) and as 'everything the *Daily Mail* is terrified of' (*Kerrang! Magazine*). Her recent publications include *Fishing in the Aftermath* (poetry) and *Springfield Road* (memoirs).

Her poem printed here is previously unpublished.

SANDIE CRAIGIE was one of Edinburgh's most gifted poets and a power-ful reader of her own work. She worked with Kevin Williamson as Assistant Editor of *Rebel Inc.* magazine in the early 90s and was a stalwart of the poetry scenes at The Yellow Café, Clutha Vaults, and so many fine and cultured venues. When she died in 2005, at the age of just forty-one, she left behind a legion of admirers but very little printed work. Now Red Squirrel have published *Coogit Bairns: Selected Prose & Poetry* (2015), a posthumous collection of her work, which has grown in reputation with the passing of the years.

The poems included here are reprinted (with much love and respect) from *Coogit Bairns*.

SOPHIE COOKE produces film-poems, site-specific poems and text poems. Film-poems include *Byland*, commissioned for the Year of Natural Scotland (2013), and *Salt*, commissioned for the Commonwealth Games culture programme (2014). Her poem 'Star' was written for live reading in an installation at the Fruitmarket Gallery (2015). She works with composers, and has read at festivals in Scotland, China, Kyrgyzstan, Ukraine and Eastern Europe. www.sophiecooke.com.

'Hermony' and 'The Cleidin is a Civilisin Mission' were first published in *Look Up Glasgow* (Freight Books, 2013).

WAYNE PRICE lives in Aberdeen. He has published a short story collection, *Furnace*, and a novel, *Mercy Seat,* with Freight Books. His recent pamphlet collection of poetry, *Fossil Record* (Smith | Doorstop) is a Laureate's Choice.

'The Lovers' was a finalist in the Manchester Poetry Competition 2014, and appeared on their website. 'The Moustache' is previously unpublished.

The other half of *#UntitledTwo* is the Neu! Reekie! compilation album
exclusively for you, yes, YOU, the lush purchaser of this book.
Because we love you and you're special.

Your digital compilation album includes tracks by:

Admiral Fallow
Bang Dirty
BMX Bandits
Boots for Dancing
Broken Records
By The Sea
Cambridge & Napier
Craig Lithgow
Ette
Eugene Kelly featuring Carla Easton
Eyes of Others
The Filthy Tongues featuring Paul Hullah
Fiona Soe Paing
FOUND
Free School Sound
FiniTribe
Gareth Sager et Norbert Woodbine
Hector Bizerk
I AM PLUTO
Kathryn Joseph
Lisa Alma
RM Hubbert & Anneliese Mackintosh
Ross Sinclair
JD Twitch & Tam Dean Burn
Tenniscoats
The Pastels
Vic Godard
WHITE
Withered Hand

To get your exclusive download code email untitledtwo@birlinn.co.uk
and say, 'Hello! Can I get my free double album?' It's that simple.

Peace & love,
Kevin & Michael x